Memorials
of
Sarah Childress Polk

Mrs. James K. Polk
1882

Memorials
of
Sarah Childress Polk

By

Anson and Fanny Nelson

Published by American Political Biography Press
Newtown, CT

All publications of
AMERICAN POLITICAL BIOGRAPHY PRESS
Are dedicated to my wife
Ellen and our two children
Katherine and William II

This particular book is
Dedicated to:

Hillary Rodham Clinton

PREFATORY NOTE.

MANY sketches and articles concerning Mrs. Polk were written during the long period of her appearance in public, and also in the years when she lived in comparative seclusion. It is deemed fitting, however, that a more full and connected account of her life should now be given, not only to those who were her familiar friends and acquaintance, but to the many others in all parts of the country who, through a long period of years have looked up to her as a type of true womanhood. For this labor of love the writers have had abundant opportunity, in the course of a long acquaintance, to observe minutely her life, character, and methods of thought in weekly visits made to Polk Place, which for more than thirty years were interrupted only by sickness or by occasional absence from the city, together with free access to all the materials necessary to make up the present narrative.

Mrs. Polk's example of womanly purity and dignity is a valuable legacy to the country. Her modesty, her self-control, her unpretentious demeanor in the highest station, her jealous care for the rights and feelings of others, her unfailing respect for the simple yet grand institutions of the country, and her unbroken reverence for all things sacred, are models worthy of imitation by all her countrywomen.

In endeavoring to set forth a simple, yet faithful and true semblance of Mrs. Polk, nothing has been said that did not seem to add to the delineation. Many apparently trifling incidents have been put in as touches to give tone and softening and roundness to the picture, which might otherwise appear bare or crude. The bits of history and biography interspersed in the narrative also seemed needful as a proper background to the portrait.

CONTENTS.

———◆———

CHAPTER VII.

CHAPTER XIII.

ILLUSTRATIONS.

SCHOOL DAYS.

SARAH CHILDRESS POLK.

CHAPTER I.

1803–1819.

SARAH CHILDRESS was born in Rutherford County, Tennessee, on the 4th of September, 1803, in the country home of her parents, Joel and Elizabeth Childress. Her mother was a Whitsitt, and belonged to a large family, well known in this and other States. Mr. and Mrs. Childress were among the early settlers of Middle Tennessee, and were persons of high standing in those days, when character was esteemed for its intrinsic merit, and when the vision of the people was less confused with the glare of place and power and wealth than now.

Mr. Childress was a successful man of business, and possessed uncommon sagacity and rare energy and enterprise. His family lived in the ease which a competency gives. Their dwelling was a " wooden

frame," but it was as good and comfortable as any
country house at that time. In speaking of her
parents, Mrs. Polk often said: " At that early day,
they had limited advantages for education, but were
enterprising and industrious, and acquired means
and property, and educated their children." She
also expressed the thought that they were fully
equal to the people of the present age, who are
better instructed and more widely informed; inasmuch as in making good use of all the aids at hand,
their minds were as much strengthened, and their
judgment as true and unbiassed, and they accomplished in reality as much as those who now work
with the help of a wider knowledge and experience.
They gave to their sons and daughters not only
the material benefit of wealth, but the more substantial and precious possession of an excellent education, the heritage of a good name, and high moral
character.

Murfreesborough, the county seat, was about two
miles distant. It had, at that time, only a Presbyterian church, a tavern, and a few stores and shops.
As is usual in small towns, the tavern was not very
attractive, and Mr. Childress often asked his friends
who were staying in Murfreesborough to spend the
night at his house. Among those who were frequently the recipients of his thoughtful hospitality

were Judge Felix Grundy, Judge Overton, Mr. Trimble, and other lawyers and men of reputation. One year Judge Crabb was his guest during the entire term of the court, and Mrs. Crabb was also there a part of the time. When they returned to Nashville they took with them Mr. Childress's two daughters, that the little girls might enjoy a visit to another town.

Canon Farrar says: " Anecdotes of infancy, incidents of childhood, indications of future greatness in boyish years, are a very rare phenomenon in ancient literature." Sarah Childress's early youth was passed in tranquillity and happiness. It was like the easy and blissful life of him concerning whom King Solomon wrote: " He shall not much remember the days of his life; because God answereth him in the joy of his heart."

There were at that time a few good schools for boys in Tennessee, but the education of girls was left to the wisdom of their parents, and to the few teachers that attempted the work here and there. In various parts of the country there was still found the fast-fading remnant of that false and injurious opinion, once almost universal, that a girl does not need a thorough education. It was thought that all learning above the necessary attainments of reading, writing, and the first principles of arithmetic,

was absolutely hurtful, disqualifying her for the
obvious duties of her station, — the care of the
household. For a short time the two girls, Sarah
and her sister Susan, went with their brothers to
the common school. Subsequently their parents
engaged the services of Mr. Samuel P. Black, the
principal of the Murfreesborough Academy, a
school for boys. He gave them lessons in the
afternoon, when the exercises of the Academy were
over for the day. They used the blackboard, and
maps and globes, and were thoroughly drilled in
the difficult beginnings of learning.

When Sarah was twelve or thirteen years old she
and her sister were sent to Nashville, to attend the
private school of Mr. Abercrombie, a noted teacher
of that day. They also took lessons on the piano
from his daughter. This was a rare accomplishment for that early time, the facilities for which
gave a peculiar reputation to the school.

General Jackson was then living in Nashville.
He was in the zenith of his military glory, and his
adopted city rejoiced in the lustre reflected upon
her by this distinguished citizen. The little pupils
were boarding in the family of Colonel Butler, one
of his staff officers, and so saw him frequently. Mrs.
Polk remembered distinctly a very brilliant ball in
the General's house, at which she was a guest.

An elderly lady who a few years since appealed to Mrs. Polk for sympathy in her desire that the simplicity and plain dressing of olden times should be restored, was surprised by the reply that she had never practised the severe plainness of which the lady spoke; that from her earliest recollection she had been dressed in silks and satins of delicate texture, in beautiful designs and colors, and had never known, even in childhood, what it was to be simply clothed, or to long for splendor of raiment, having always possessed it. She did not believe that the apparel in old times was plainer than it is now, but that the means to possess this luxury were then limited to fewer individuals.

After a year or two spent in home study and private lessons, and when Sarah was about fifteen years old, she was sent with her sister to the Moravian Female Academy in Salem, North Carolina. Mr. and Mrs. Childress desired their daughters to have the advantage of a large school, not only in its more comprehensive course of study, but in that deeper, keener, intellectual quickening that comes from fellowship in culture.

The little town of Salem was founded by the Society of the United Brethren, about the middle of the eighteenth century, under the direction of Count Zinzendorf, from whom it received its name, meaning "peace." The "quaint, quiet, green old town" lies a thousand feet above the level of the sea, in an undulating, beautifully wooded country. "From the more elevated points, not remote from this unique town, the Pilot Mountain may be seen, with its castellated peak, rising three hundred feet above the shoulders of the mountain, and bearing a striking resemblance to an antiquated Gothic castle, such as greets the eye on the Rhine; and still beyond, on a clear day, the practised eye can detect the steel-blue rim of the remoter mountain ranges that form such a conspicuous feature in Western North Carolina. There still the old town of Salem stands, with its antique dwellings, tile roofs, low eaves, and cramped little attics, unchanged in many of its aspects amid all the changes that have occurred around it. There it stands, with its primitive customs, its peculiar religious services, its pious Moravian Brethren, its benevolent institutions." [1]

Here stood the Female Academy, a healthful and peculiarly suitable retreat for the calm and studious life of young girls. Under the charge of this religious society, of acknowledged piety and elevation of character, the great usefulness and success of the Salem Academy were assured,

[1] Rev. J. E. Edwards.

as its nine long decades have proved. Many of
its pupils had braved the toils and dangers of a
long journey to share in its advantages. "The
only uniform worn by the pupils in this old
Moravian school was a neat and closely fitting
lace cap. It was a striking feature. Sweet, ruddy
faces peered out from the quilted borders of this
handsome and decidedly tasteful piece of head-
gear. That of the larger girls was trimmed with
white ribbon, the smaller girls with pink. It was
a beautiful spectacle on Examination-Day, as the
annual closing day of the session was called, to
see one hundred and fifty or two hundred girls,
dressed in white, with flowing sashes and flaunt-
ing ribbons, and each attired with the tidy cap,
marching in procession from the Academy to the
church." [1]

Upon their starting, Mr. Childress gave to each
of his daughters a French gold coin, a louis d'or,
worth about four dollars and eighty-four cents, as
a parting gift. This piece of money, so likely to
find its way speedily into other hands, Mrs. Polk
preserved through many years and vicissitudes,
until the end of her life, and it is now a much-
prized relic.

The young girls traversed the hundreds of miles

[1] Rev. J. E. Edwards.

between Murfreesborough and Salem on horseback,
escorted by their elder brother, Anderson Childress,
and attended by a trusty man-servant who carried
their portmanteaus on his horse. He belonged to
a class no longer in existence. In the domestic
economy of those times, which the vast changes
wrought in the last thirty-odd years have con-
signed to the past, among the slaves of every
rich man there could be found some intelligent
and faithful ones who possessed the implicit confidence of their master and friend.

Such a trip in these days of swift and easy travel,
more than seventy years afterward, would seem like
a series of romantic adventures. But it would be
a romance from which the exciting element of
danger was eliminated, leaving it gently stirring
and thoroughly agreeable. Far different were the
circumstances forty or fifty years still earlier, when
the pioneers of Middle Tennessee, dauntless and
heroic, were journeying through this wilderness to
the land which loomed before their prophetic eyes
like an enchanting mirage, blooming as a garden
of roses, remote in time, not space. Then they
were shadowed by the Indians, and often assaulted,
suffering the severest privations and hardships. It was not so with our young travellers,
who had nothing to fear from the rude and cruel

warriors of the forest, and to whose youthful and inexperienced fancy, the cool, green shades on either side of the road suggested only pleasant visions of noonday rest and refreshment.

No views are more varied and picturesque than those through which their way was taken. It lay over a rolling country, with charming views of hill and dale; and through woods thickly peopled with the descendants of the ancient families of oak, beech, hickory, walnut, cedar, wild-cherry, willow, and many others radiant in rustling garments of every shade of green, and with branches bending to the whisperings of the wind. There was the stir of many kinds of animal life; the hum of insects; the clear, sweet notes of birds flitting hither and thither in gleaming plumage; the soft beauty of sky; and the indescribable variety and charm which nature bestows in the favored climate of Tennessee and North Carolina. The forests were already decking themselves in color when our little travellers rode through them. After riding all day some friendly farmhouse would give them shelter and rest, and the knowledge of a domestic life entirely new to them. They crossed the broad, beautiful, majestic Holston, now the Tennessee river; the wild, picturesque French Broad, which

the Indians called the Tahkeeostee river; and
other streams, smaller but not less pleasing in
their gracefulness.

An entirely new and different life awaited Sarah
and her sister in their transient home in the Salem
Academy. The hush and method of a large school,
the lessons learned with the stimulus of the small
world of students, the pleasant walks and talks
with many new friends, congenial and beloved,
the daily services for prayer and divine guidance,
all helped to mould the growing character of Sarah
Childress. On Sunday morning, the girls met in
their respective class-rooms to receive what was
called Bible instruction. A verse from Scripture
to be memorized had been assigned the previous
Sunday, and it was expected that the chapter from
which that verse was taken would be read by the
pupils in their rooms during the week. After the
recitation by each one in turn, the entire chapter
was read aloud and commented on by the teacher.

In after years one of the teachers wrote as follows: " Let us recall some of our own peculiar and
particular enjoyments. As the end of the year
drew near, busy hands and heads were occupied
in preparing for the Christmas times, — the decorations, the dialogues, all having reference to the

babe in Bethlehem's manger, whose birth we were commemorating. Then came the old year's closing meeting, held in our Academy Chapel, followed by the watch-meeting at midnight in the church, which we attended with the Salem congregation, and a few hours later the New Year's sermon in the morning."

While at school in Salem, Sarah did a little piece of needle-work which she fortunately kept during all the succeeding years. It is the picture of a tomb gleaming white through the foliage of surrounding trees, and is worked in chenille on a white satin ground. It is skilfully and delicately done, the different shades of green, brown, and yellow blending naturally. In later life Mrs. Polk herself called attention to a resemblance which struck us as having in it something prophetic. It bears a remarkable likeness to the tomb in the garden on the east of the house, in full view of her chamber window, which for more than forty years was the reminder of her joys and sorrows, and which became, as the months glided by, her daily reminder of the blissful reunion awaiting her in the near future.

These tranquil days of study, of girlish dreamings and anticipations, came suddenly to an end. Sarah and her sister were called home by the illness and death of their father. They did not return to the Academy, and Sarah occupied herself with the duties of home and social life, and with the sacred charge of helping to comfort her mother.

Mr. Childress left a good estate to his family.

HOME LIFE AND MARRIAGE.

CHAPTER II.

1820–1825.

THERE were many friends and admirers who sought the companionship and a share in the sunny society of Mrs. Childress's household. Among them was James Knox Polk, whose ancestors came to America from the north of Ireland, early in the eighteenth century. Their name was originally Pollock, but the wearing action of pronunciation reduced it in the course of time to Poll'k, and finally to the present name. Mr. Polk was born in Mecklenburg County, North Carolina, November 2, 1795, and came to Tennessee with his father's family in early life. He was a practitioner of the law, and at that time principal clerk in the senatorial branch of the legislature, which met at Murfreesborough, then the capital of the State. In the public estimation he was a young man of mark, and very soon after was elected to the legislature to represent Maury County, the place of his residence, and was subsequently chosen by Governor

Carroll as one of his staff officers. He was then about twenty-seven years old; very youthful in appearance, but with a fine presence, though not commanding in stature. With quiet manners, he was still courteous and dignified. His own high self-respect and unswerving rectitude were shown in the respect he habitually paid to the rights and feelings of others. These sterling qualities attained their full development when in the succeeding years of power they had ample room to expand, and their strength and beneficence were so often apparent.

The beauty and magnetic presence of the young girl, whose worth, dignity, and modest reserve, tempered by the graces of playful wit and ready repartee, formed so striking a counterpart or complement to his own character, made an indelible impression upon the young lawyer. His labors at the Court House where the legislature convened, were charmingly alternated with visits to Miss Childress. His attentions were favorably received and ended in an engagement of marriage. He laughingly said to her that had he remained the clerk of the legislature she would never have consented to marry him!

In 1880 Capt. John W. Childress, a nephew of Mrs. Polk's, presented to the Tennessee Historical Society the original license issued by the clerk of the County Court of Rutherford County, authorizing the celebration of the marriage relation between James Knox Polk and Sarah Childress. On Thursday evening, the 1st of January, 1824, the marriage ceremony was performed by the Rev. Dr. Henderson, pastor of the Presbyterian church.

A numerous company of guests did honor to the occasion, and it was, as a great-granddaughter of Mrs. Childress says, "a large country wedding." One of that merry gathering, Mrs. Daniel Graham, who was Miss Maria McIver, and at whose nuptials Mrs. Polk had been a bridesmaid, lived to see the young bride attain the age of eighty-two years. The bride and groom were attended by four young couples, among whom were Aaron V. Brown and Lucius J. Polk. The history of the former bears such a resemblance to that of Mr. Polk, that it was singularly fitting he should be one of the next and best friends on this occasion. They were both graduates of the University of North Carolina at Chapel Hill, and were partners in the practice of the law. Mr. Brown was often a member of the Tennessee legislature, and a representative in Congress five or six years, until 1845, when he was elected Governor of Tennessee. In 1857 he was Postmaster-General in the Cabinet of President Buchanan. In various parts of the country he was frequently mentioned as a candidate for the presidency. His life, also, was cut short in its prime, for he lived not quite ten years longer than his illustrious friend.

Festivities in honor of the marriage were the order of the day. Friday evening, January 2, a large party was given the young couple at Mrs. Lytle's. The bride remembered that on this occasion she wore a blue embroidered silk. The next evening an entertainment took place at the house of Mrs. Dr. Rucker, the sister of the bride; and on Monday evening they were invited to a large party at Mrs. Wendell's. Tuesday, they were under the uupleasant necessity of declining the compliment of a dinner at Mrs. McCullough's, because they were obliged to leave for Columbia, where a company of guests had been asked by the parents of the bridegroom to meet them the following Thursday evening. The high waters usual in midwinter made travelling somewhat difficult and uncertain, and it was important, therefore, to start early, that they might be sure to arrive in time to receive the greetings of those who were to meet in their honor at Columbia.

This beautiful town, the county seat of Maury County, " the garden of Tennessee," is situated in one of earth's favored regions, and is as fertile as the far-famed blue-grass counties of Kentucky. This happy spot was the home of Mr. Polk's relatives, and the young couple lived in a cottage in their midst, the bride receiving from them not only agreeable and acceptable attentions, but gentle and affectionate regard, as a welcome and beloved member of her husband's family. She retained their kind consideration as long as they lived.

Surrounded by loving friends, the honeymoon and many following moons passed swiftly away. Smoothly and noiselessly the social and domestic machinery of life ran on with its innumerable wheels, delicate and closely interdependent, and the days and weeks slipped by without chronicle. But the wedded pair were not drifting idly with the stream. Their character gradually expanded, unfolded, and rose under the mutually stimulating, helpful, and elevating power of thoroughly congenial daily intercourse, in which one was exactly complemented by the other.

After the marriage of her daughter, Mrs. Childress went to Murfreesborough, exchanging her interest in the farm for a house and lot in town. There she lived until her death, refusing to give up the old-fashioned home with its large rooms and ample grounds, for the more modern house with modern conveniences, to which in her old age her children urged her to move.

General Lafayette the friend of the American

Colonies, reached Nashville early in May, 1825, in the course of his triumphal progress through the United States. He was received with every mark of high esteem, and a few days after his arrival a grand ball was given in his honor. The hotels were overrun with visitors, and Mr, and Mrs. Polk were entertained at the house of their friend, Mr. John Catron, a leading lawyer of the city. The tickets of invitation, which had been sent out some weeks before, are remarkably elaborate and artistic for the capital of what was then a western State, so near the confines of civilization. They reveal an enthusiastic regard for the magnanimous foreigner who had done so much for our country. They were printed on fine paper, eight by ten inches. On either side of the page is engraved a large fluted column. That on the right is surmounted with a bust of Lafayette, inscribed with his name, and is intwined with a broad ribbon on which are the names of his battles; the dates 1777–81 are on the base of the pedestal, around which lie cannon, balls, drums, torches, etc. The column on the left is similarly decorated with a bust of Jackson, and inscribed with the names of his battles, bearing the dates 1813–15. These pillars are united by a strip of sky holding the thirteen stars, in the centre of which at the top of the arch, appears the blazing

sun with the date "'76" in the disk. The strip of
sky is bounded above by a garland of oak-leaves and
acorns. Just beneath the sun hovers the American
eagle with the familiar emblems, the bunch of
arrows and the branch of peace. In its beak is a
laurel wreath which it is placing upon the head of
Washington's bust. This rests upon a fluted column
rising out of the clouds, and is surrounded with
guns, spears, swords, banners, and the cap of liberty.
Below are the words in large capitals, "Welcome
Lafayette!" In the remaining space between the
pillars is printed the invitation to the ball, signed by
the names of the twelve managers, who were among
the chief citizens of Nashville. This design, full of
patriotic pride, was the work of R. E. W. Earle,
who lived at the Hermitage and painted many portraits of Jackson, his beloved and honored patron.
The painter's grave is only a few feet from the well-
known tomb of the General, and is covered with a
slab bearing this epitaph: "Artist, Friend, and
Companion of General Andrew Jackson."

The ball was given at the Nashville Inn, the
principal hotel, and among those present were Mr.
and Mrs. Polk, who had come from Columbia in
honor of the noble Frenchman and revolutionary
hero. This grand entertainment shared the usual
fate of all celebrations prepared on so extensive a

scale. The most vivid remembrance it has left is not of the distinguished guests, nor of the brilliant assemblage, nor of the graceful and splendid picture it presented, but of the crowd and the crush, which were so uncomfortable as to obscure all other recollections.

A WIDER LIFE.

CHAPTER III.

1825–1833.

MR. POLK assiduously attended to the duties of his profession, practising law in the courts of Maury and the adjoining counties. During the long periods later in life when he was busily engaged with the cares of government, as member of Congress or Governor of Tennessee, and until he became President of the United States, the practice of his profession was only suspended. As soon as his term of office expired, he returned with ardor to the pursuit of his chosen calling. It was one of his maxims that a man should never abandon his profession, and if called away for a time, should return to it as soon as possible.

His talents and force of character continued to win the esteem and confidence of his fellow-citizens; and when he became a candidate for Congress his active canvass was successful. In 1825 he was elected to represent the district composed of the counties of Giles, Maury, Lincoln, and Bedford, in

the Congress of the United States. This was a
high distinction at that time.

The Hon. A. O. P. Nicholson had always known
Mr. Polk. "They were near neighbors, belonged
to the same profession, were members of the same
political family, and closely identified with the political conflicts of each successive year." In the
following extract Judge Nicholson speaks of that
whereof he knew: —

"At the election in 1825 Mr. Polk was chosen
a member of Congress, after a most arduous and
warmly contested canvass. In this canvass, the
peculiar traits of his character were prominently
developed. His competitors were men of age, experience, and intelligence. He was young, and
comparatively inexperienced and unknown. It was
a contest to be decided mainly upon personal
popularity. The people were not then divided
into two great political parties. The candidates
all professed the same general political faith.
The chances at the outset were decidedly against
him, but he had set his heart upon success, and
he resolved to attain it. The district was large,
but he traversed and canvassed it again and again.
Before the canvass was half over he had displayed
so much activity and energy in his movements, and
had instilled into his supporters so much of his

own ardent zeal that he was regarded by each of
his competitors as the most formidable opponent.
In his public speeches there was always an earnest-
ness and sincerity of manner which was peculiarly
impressive. He seemed ever to feel what he said,
and to speak with an animation and ardor which
flowed from his heart. This was the secret of his
success as a popular orator. He was persuasive
because he spoke from his heart as well as from
his head. His superior tact in illustrating his
positions by humorous anecdotes, of which he had
stored away in his capacious memory very many,
while he was always courteous and mild and
respectful, aided him to win the predilections of
his hearers. As the canvass approached its termination he displayed all the skill of a veteran general
in marshalling his forces for an impending battle.
He dashed from point to point over his district
with a rapidity which struck his opponents with
surprise, and paralyzed them with despair. He
infused into his own friends the same ardor and
energy which actuated himself. When the election
came on he was triumphantly successful."

In the autumn of 1825, leaving his wife in the
quiet cottage-home in Columbia, Mr. Polk started
on horseback, with Colonel Allen and several
other members of Congress, who were travelling to

Washington. At Baltimore they took the stage-
coach, and left their horses there until their return
in March. When Mr. Polk went again to Washington, in the autumn of 1826, he was accompanied by his wife. The roads were rough, and
the fatigues of the long journey very great, but
such obstacles could not deter her. The strength,
buoyant spirits, and easy courage of youth enabled
her to enjoy all the pleasures, and to make light
of the toils by the way. The horizon of a wider
life and a more extended prospect now stretched
its dim outline before her,— the soft tints and misty
shapes of earth and sky blending till she could
scarcely discern where the ceaseless endeavor of
the one was met by the perfect peace of the
other. So in her future, the exalted influences of
success, joy, and content, were to mingle with all
her earthly experiences. The pleasant village
occupations and associations were displaced by
the unknown companionships and events of new
and untried scenes.

They travelled in their own carriage, attended by
two of their colored servants, a man and a maid,
and thus accomplished the long and difficult journey, — resting at night in some farmhouse, and
enjoying by day the scenery and changes by the
way. They were accompanied by General Sam

Houston, and at Knoxville were joined by Judge Hugh L. White. It was in November, and the golden sunshine and brilliant colors of October had vanished, leaving the soft, silvery haze of mid-autumn, when a spirit of memory or reverie seems to hover in the air and to impress the landscape with its dreamy quietude.

The grand old wildwood solitudes lay, for miles at a time, on both sides of the way. A great part of the country through which they passed had once been the immense hunting-grounds of the Choctaw, the Cherokee, the Creek, and other tribes of Indians, who occupied the vast and rich lands extending from the Ohio to the Tennessee River on the west and south, and eastward to the Cumberland Mountains. These forests of magnificent poplars, elms, sycamores, locusts, maples, cottonwoods, oaks, and numerous other trees, among which were the smaller growths of dogwood, holly, laurel, etc., had been held by the dusky warriors as a common territory for killing game, and were grandly enclosed by the mighty waters of these two majestic rivers, and the steep mountain fastnesses. Undeveloped and undreamed of by these careless rovers lay its great wealth of resources in minerals, and its treasures which the magic wand of industry and knowledge was to call forth in coming years. When our travellers were leisurely journeying through this attractive region the picturesque tribes had departed, leaving comparatively few traces of their ancient reign other than the peculiar and musical names they had given to flowing rivers and wide tracts of country.

Arriving at Washington, Mr. and Mrs. Polk took temporary lodgings at Williamson's Hotel on Pennsylvania Avenue. The streets and pavements were far from what they now are; the architecture of the public buildings and private dwellings was simplicity itself compared with the present structures. But Washington was nevertheless a delightful city, notwithstanding its physical deficiencies, for then as now it was a centre of learning, refinement, and activity, — the capital of the nation.

In the third decade of the century it was seldom that the members of Congress occupied their own or hired house during their transient stay in the capital; and frequently two or more families would "mess" together. This camp phrase means that several of them would engage apartments in the same house, in which there was a dining-room and parlor set apart for their special use. This arrangement secured something of the privacy of home with its congenial company and pleasant daily intercourse. In this way, at various times, Mr. and Mrs. Polk were the companions of the Hon. Hugh Lawson White, Senator from Tennessee, the Hon. Mr. Jarvis of Maine, the Hon. John C. Calhoun of South Carolina, and others. Mrs. Polk's strong understanding and sound sense, the winning gifts and graces of her person and character, were readily recognized, and she soon became a favorite with all.

It was the central period of President John Quincy Adams's administration. The public mind was not agitated by any great political question, and the social life of the capital city flowed pleasantly on. This tranquillity, however, had for a short time been disturbed by the duel between Randolph and Clay in the spring of 1826. The declining health of Mrs. Adams permitted her no longer to appear in general society, except at public receptions in the White House, where she presided with the animation and gracious dignity which had made her supremacy so potent when Mr. Adams was Secretary of State.

Mrs. Polk's preference was for the Presbyterian church, the choice of her parents, whose ministry had been her religious guide, except when under the charge of the Moravians at Salem. Her husband made a point of going with her to religious services, and they became regular attendants in the congregation of the First Presbyterian Church, on Four and a-half Street, of which the Rev. Dr. Post was then the pastor.

When the session of Congress closed, they returned to their cottage-home in Columbia. She varied the quiet enjoyments of home with visits to her mother and other relatives in Murfrees-borough; and he devoted himself to the political canvass, having again become a candidate for Congress; and after a severe contest with a formidable competitor, was re-elected. Thenceforward until 1839, when he voluntarily ceased to be a candidate, he was chosen every two years, and served his fellow-citizens in the deliberations of the National Assembly with signal ability and faithfulness. Thus for fourteen consecutive years the duties of his high office fixed his residence in Washington during the winter months. The summers were spent at home in Tennessee. In the annual trips, different routes were taken, thus gaining variety and much pleasant information. Sometimes they went by stage-coach through East Tennessee and Virginia, *via* Fredericksburg, — on one occasion, in a carriage to Lexington, Kentucky, going from there by the Maysville route to the Ohio River, taking the steamer to Wheeling, and the stage to Washington. Another time they returned by way of New York City, thence to Albany, by the Erie Canal to Buffalo, from there to the Niagara Falls, and thence homeward. In this circuitous route they saw different phases of life; and enjoyed even the tedious progress of the canal-boat, which gave ample time to gaze upon and to admire the panorama of fine and varied landscapes. Mrs. Polk had neither care nor trouble about any travelling arrangements, and enjoyed all the journeys. It made little difference to her whether the accommodations were good or not, she was thoroughly satisfied with the pleasure, and made light of whatever hardship might befall.

On one occasion, while travelling in the Virginia mountains, the stage was overturned and several gentlemen injured. Mr. Lyon, a senator, who was one of the passengers, said to her, "Put your foot in my hand, Madame, and I will help you out." She did so, and came out of the wreck unhurt, not understanding how it could be, but still thankful for the deliverance.

Another incident occurred near Columbia. The stage-driver ventured into a swollen stream, when the horses got into deep water and began to swim. An inch or two more, and the stage would have been engulfed. A man coming up the bank on

horseback, cried to the driver to stop. Mr. Polk,
who could not swim, called out from his seat
within the stage, offering a reward of any amount
of money that might be named, if somebody would
save his wife. The man on horseback seemed too
much frightened to grasp the opportunity, and
Mr. Granville Pillow, who was sitting beside Mrs.
Polk, throwing his coat down on the seat, exclaimed,
"I will take you out, Madame!" Swimming to the
bank and compelling the man to give up his horse,
he mounted, and plunging into the rapid current,
came up behind the stage, and asking her to step
upon the high hind wheel, and then upon the
shoulder of the horse, he held her firmly in his
arms and bore her safely to the bank. She did
not even get her feet damp.

During the session of 1830–1831 she remained
at home in Columbia, but greatly missed the cheer
of Mr. Polk's companionship. One day, much de-
pressed, a friend playfully asked why she did not
go to Washington, instead of staying at home and
wearing so long a face.

"I stayed at home," she returned, "to save
money to make a display upon next winter."
This was only pleasantry. She had no occasion
to save, for her husband had a lucrative practice,
and was not dependent upon his salary.

The following letter was written just before the close of the session. It is on a large, square sheet of paper, folded and sealed in the old style, when envelopes were unknown, and is addressed to her at Columbia, bearing his Congressional frank. It affords a glimpse of the manners of the time.

WASHINGTON CITY, March 2d, 1831.

MY DEAR SARAH, — I write you from my seat in the Hall at an evening session. It is now between eight and nine o'clock at night; the Hall is splendidly lighted up, as is usual at an evening session, and the lobbies are crowded with ladies and spectators. We will probably sit until midnight and very probably later. At what hour tomorrow we shall adjourn I can form no opinion, but I hope in time to enable us to get to Baltimore to-morrow.

I will add a postscript to this letter in the morning before I seal and mail it, and it will be of course the last that I will write you, before I hope to see you. I will run a race home with this letter, and think I shall beat it. I know I shall if I have luck with the stages and steamboats.

Very affectionately, your husband,

JAMES K. POLK.

N. B.   House Repts., March 3d, 1831.

The House sat until four o'clock this morning,
and have just met again, it being now eleven
o'clock.   About two o'clock I became so much
worn down and fatigued, that for the first time
during my service here, I found myself compelled
to go to my lodgings.   I feel rather in low spirits
this morning, for I fear that the House may sit to
so late an hour as to prevent me from reaching
Baltimore for to-morrow's stage.   I will, however,
leave, at all events, in time to get there, unless
there should be some matter of paramount im-
portance to render it indispensable for us to remain.   I will get off if I can with any sort of
propriety.

Very affectionately, your husband,

JAMES K. POLK.

In 1833 Mr. and Mrs. Polk went in their private
carriage through Virginia to Washington.   On the
night of November 13–14 they were at a country
house near Wytheville, when the grand meteoric
display of that year took place.   Early in the
morning, before they were up, a servant came in
to make a fire, and said in reply to some question
about the time of day, "Ole Miss 's been up a long

time, scared nearly to death. The sky's fallin' and the day of judgment's come."

Mr. Polk stepped out as soon as possible, but the fast coming dawn prevented his seeing much of the astonishing spectacle. Mr. Edward E. Barnard, the well-known astronomer of Vanderbilt University, afterward of Lick Observatory in California, says: "You have read of the wonderful display of November, 1833, when the heavens flashed and flamed with countless myriads of burning stars, as plentiful in their fiery descent as the flakes of a December snowstorm. Ah! That was a wonderful sight. How we love to listen to our grandfathers and grandmothers, as they expatiate on the wonders of that awful night when God's long patience seemed to have come to an end, and the day of wrath near its dawn. Was it not enough to shed terror in the soul of the timid, when the whole canopy of heaven seemed falling in one ceaseless rain of fire? And what a dawn was that, when the great sun showed himself in the eastern sky, blotting out with his mellow beams that night of terror. But there were those during that night in whose hearts the thought of terror never entered, and who with weariless eyelids watched until the dawn — to them how unwelcome — paled the glorious sight. How different in

knowing and not knowing the cause of this superb
phenomenon!"

The artist Earle had spent some time with General Jackson at the White House. During his stay
there the Tennesseans who were assembled one
evening in the parlor of Mr. and Mrs. Polk proposed that they should have their portraits painted
by him, and this proposition was soon carried into
effect. Mrs. Polk's portrait, the earliest one of her,
has preserved her youthful appearance, with the
bright eyes, and raven hair hanging in clustering
curls around the face. It has justly been called
the picture of a bride, for the freshness of youth
clung to her for many years.

Mr. Polk was much opposed to banks, and had
taken strong ground with General Jackson against
irresponsible paper currency, and in favor of the
exclusive use of gold and silver as a circulating
medium. He was consistent, and used specie in
the payment of all his debts. The opposition of
General Jackson and his party to the United States
Bank, and indeed to all banks, created great excitement throughout the country for several years, and
was a prolific theme of Congressional debate, and
in all public speech on political occasions. There
was a time when the currency of each State was at
a small discount in the adjoining States, and this

irregularity and loss to travellers and others gave force to the arguments of those who advocated specie payments in all business transactions.

On a journey to Washington Mr. and Mrs. Polk had rested during the night, as usual. Early one morning, just as everything was ready, and the trunks were locked, Mr. Polk entered in haste, and said, " Sarah, get some money out of the trunk. I haven't enough in my pocket to pay expenses during the day."

With a little flush of excitement, being much hurried, she opened a trunk and began turning up the clothing, in one corner and then in another, to find the bags of specie packed in different places. " Don't you see," she exclaimed, " how trouble-some it is to carry around gold and silver? This is enough to show you how useful banks are."

" Sarah, you've turned your politics, then," he rejoined; " but all I want now is that money."

They were accompanied by a party of Congress-men and friends, and when seated in the coach Mr. Polk related with considerable embellishment and humor the incident that had just occurred. It was apparent that his wife had taken sides against him on the Bank question. All clapped their hands, and were so boisterous in their mirth that the driver, leaning from his seat on the box, asked,

"What is the matter, gentlemen? What are you laughing at?"

Several of the party, who held opinions in opposition to those of Mr. Polk, were much pleased and amused at the idea of his wife sympathizing with them.

Not long after this, when a notable Virginian, whose opinions coincided with those of Mr. Polk, was calling upon them, she remarked, "Mr. Polk, you and your friends certainly are mistaken about that Bank question. Why, if we must use gold and silver all the time, a lady can scarcely carry enough money with her."

The visitor laughed, and Mr. Polk told her afterward that their Virginia friend would certainly conclude that she was not quite right politically.

LIFE IN WASHINGTON.

CHAPTER IV.

1834–1839.

IN the summer of 1834, at her home in Columbia, Mrs. Polk came to the conclusion, toward which her wishes and meditations had long been tending, to unite with the church. Speaking of this decision to no one but her husband's mother, who was " a strict church-woman," — a Presbyterian — she was surprised on the following Sunday to hear it announced from the pulpit that the door of the church was open for the admission of members, and surprised still more to find that she herself was the only candidate. So pleased was Mr. Polk's mother with this decision that she had brought about its immediate accomplishment by making arrangements for it with Mr. Larrabee, the pastor.

While Mr. Polk was in the habit of attending church with his wife, it often happened that as the hour for services approached, he was engaged in the company of men who, either from indifference or carelessness, forgot the Sabbath and its universal obligation. As it was an awkward and difficult

thing for him to excuse himself, his wife took the
case into her own dexterous management.   Shawled
and bonneted, she would enter the room and ask
her husband and his friends to go with her to
church, saying that she did not wish to go alone.
One day in Washington, when she did this, a visitor asked, " Mrs. Polk, what is the use of going to
church ?   You Presbyterians believe that you will
be saved anyhow."

" Oh, no, sir, we believe no such thing," she
replied ; " and I wish to go particularly to-day, because Dr. B., a fine preacher, is to fill the pulpit."

" Then I would like to go with you, Madame,
for I have played cards all night with him many
a time."

Her custom of requesting her husband's Sunday
callers to accompany him and her to church soon
had the effect of dispersing them before her appearance, if they did not wish to accept the invitation.

Soon after becoming settled in Washington, Mrs.
Polk, wishing to keep up her music, procured an
instrument and an instructor and applied herself
diligently to the task.   But it was not long before
the unequal struggle became wearisome.   With the
circle of her acquaintance constantly widening, and
engagements multiplying, she was obliged to give
up the music studies.

At this point it may be well to mention a few of the ladies who were her friends and companions at that time. Mrs. General Van Ness was admired for her beauty and accomplishments, and venerated for her Christian character and beneficence. She founded the Washington City Orphan Asylum; and it is said that she was the first American woman who was buried with public honors. Her niece, Cornelia, the daughter of Cornelius Van Ness, the Chief Justice, and Governor of Vermont, spent some time with her aunt, in the winter of 1828–1829, and was a charming addition to Washington society. A few years later she married, in Paris, Mr. Roosevelt of New York, General Lafayette giving the bride away. Other friends were: the future Mrs. J. J. Crittenden, at that time Mrs. William H. Ashley, wife of the "sole representative in Congress from Missouri;" Mrs. Levi Woodbury, the wife of the Secretary of the Navy during President Jackson's administration; Mrs. Louis McLane, the wife of the Secretary of State in the same Cabinet, but who afterward became Secretary of the Treasury; Mrs. Thomas H. Benton, the daughter of Governor McDowell of Virginia; Mrs. Clay, of Alabama; Mrs. Pleasanton, of Washington; Mrs. Edward Livingston; Mrs. Jarvis, of Maine; Mrs. Lewis Cass, wife of the Secretary of War;

Mrs. Chamberlain, of New York; Mrs. Robert Y. Hayne, of South Carolina; Mrs. Robert J. Walker, of Mississippi; Mrs. Gordon, of Virginia; Mrs. Isaac Hill, of New Hampshire; Mrs. Caleb Cushing, of Massachusetts; Mrs. Rives, of Virginia; Mrs. Marcy, of New York; Mrs. R. H. Gillet; Mrs. William C. Preston and Mrs. John C. Calhoun, of South Carolina; and many others.

The custom of making social calls on New Year's Day was early introduced into Washington society. Among Mrs. Polk's recollections of the time when she was the wife of a Congressman was the New Year call of General Edmund P. Gaines. He was dressed in full regimentals, and wore at his side the sword presented to him by the Legislature of Tennessee. " Madame," said he, " I have come to call on you, and have worn in your honor my Tennessee sword."

The country was greatly disturbed in the spring of 1832 by the Black Hawk war; and two months afterward by the first appearance of the Asiatic cholera, which broke out at Quebec and swept with violence over the land, taking the course of the lakes and rivers and other principal routes of travel. General Scott's army, in vessels on the northern lakes, going to meet Black Hawk, was met and routed by the cholera, a subtler and more powerful foe than the Indian chief. In the succeeding month General Atkinson defeated Black Hawk and took him prisoner.

But the greatest excitement occurred in December of this year, and near the close of General Jackson's first term as President, when South Carolina attempted to nullify the tariff laws enacted by Congress. The whole country was in a tremor, and the President's celebrated proclamation on the subject was the theme of fierce debate in both Houses of Congress. These violent discussions were also heard on the hustings everywhere. This agitation, permeating all departments of life, influenced social affairs to a considerable extent, especially in Washington. The subject which had been under fierce discussion for three or four years reached a climax in 1832, and resulted in the increased popularity of General Jackson. He was re-elected President by an overwhelming majority, receiving two hundred and nineteen electoral votes, out of two hundred and sixty-eight cast by the electoral colleges.

It is not within the scope of the record of a woman's life, to discourse of wars and political disturbances, and weighty matters of State. They are mentioned simply to show what were the agitations of social life, arousing partisan feeling and separating friends. To avoid these dangers, not only a clear understanding and good judgment were required, but also unselfish, kindly forbearance and gentle consideration for the rights and sensibilities of others. Guided by rare discernment, prudence, and self-command, Mrs. Polk's daily intercourse was free from hasty or unkind allusions and irritating talk.

With the lowly self-estimation of love, she felt that her character had been moulded by the wise influence of her husband. She relates that, in the exuberance of spirits which had never felt the restraint of hard experiences, she would sometimes make a hasty remark, which would be instantly checked, not by a reproof, — Mr. Polk seldom told her that she did wrong, — but by a smile which she well understood to mean disapproval of her inconsiderateness.

The following incident shows her high ideal of the dignity of her position as the wife of a Congressman. The wife of a Cabinet officer wrote her that she was going to the races on that day because two prominent Tennesseans were to run their horses, both of which were noted for good blood and great speed, and that if Mrs. Polk wished to see the spectacle, she would call in her carriage at the proper hour, and take her out to the course. Mrs. Polk replied with thanks, but declined to go. In the

evening, meeting her at a party, the lady said, " Oh,
why did you not go with me to-day ? " She then
told of the large concourse, including government
officials, members of Congress, and many ladies.
Mrs. Polk answered that she declined because she
had never attended the races, and did not wish to
violate her rule.

" Well," was the laughing reply, " that is a reflection on me." " Oh, no," returned Mrs. Polk, " not
at all. You are in the habit of going. I am not."
She did not break this rule, and never saw a horse-
race. Her ideal of propriety was the counterpart
of her husband's, who had a delicate conception of
the fitness of things. He did not wish his wife even
to jest about personal incongruities, or anything
that reflected on the character or manners of others.
He would sometimes say, " Sarah, I wish you would
not say that. I understand you, but others might
not, and a wrong impression might be made."

" That," said she, " was the strongest rebuke he
ever gave me. When persons speak of my strict
ideas of propriety, I think of my husband's circum-
spection, and reply, ' You were not brought up in
so strict a school as I was.' "

Though Mr. Polk was one of the youngest members when he first took his seat in the House, he
was at the beginning of his second session made

4

chairman of the Committee on Foreign Relations.
He was not only the firm political supporter, but the
ardent personal friend of President Jackson, and
was looked upon as the leader of the Jackson forces
in the House of Representatives. Recollections of
the past undoubtedly aided to strengthen the warm
friendship always felt by General Jackson for Mr.
Polk. It is said that when young Jackson with his
mother and brother fled before the army of Corn-
wallis in the war of the Revolution, they took refuge
in Mecklenburg County, North Carolina, and lived
for some time with the neighbors and friends of Mr.
Polk's father and grandfather.

About the middle of General Jackson's second
term Mr. Polk was chosen Speaker of the House,
and held the office until his withdrawal from Congress. The responsibilities which this position imposed upon his wife were fulfilled by her with ease
and dignity, while her entertainments left many
pleasant memories. Additional rooms in the house
where they boarded were obtained for these festival
occasions. Making her apartments elastic and ex-
pansible at her pleasure, she could receive a large
party of guests at any time, without the care of an
extensive establishment.

Among her associates were Mrs. Seaton and
Mrs. Gales, although their husbands were adher-

ents of the party to which Mr. Polk was opposed.
Gales and Seaton published the "National Intel-
ligencer" for many years, and it was a prosperous paper under their control. On one occasion,
Mrs. Seaton was desirous that Mrs. Polk should
attend an entertainment she proposed giving,
and was told by Mr. Polk that his wife would be
present if he could get through with his duties
in time to escort her. She impulsively replied
that Mrs. Polk must come, whether he could
attend her or not, and that she would provide
an escort for her. Thereupon she invited Mr.
Buchanan, a bachelor senator, afterward President,
and Colonel King, another bachelor; but the lady
did not appear. When Mrs. Seaton next met
Mrs. Polk she said, "I invited those two old
Democrats to be company for you, and behold,
you did not come!"

Mrs. Polk preferred to remain at home when
her husband was too closely engaged to give
her his attendance, although there were many
gentlemen offering courtesies and desiring to
wait upon her to places of amusement. Taking
a deep interest in his patient inquiries into the
abstruse and complicated political questions of
the day, she was at pains to inform herself on
these subjects, and become familiar with the

great matters then exercising the minds of public men. But she had the intuitive tact which is rarely united with such insight and understanding, and was too delicate and reserved to proclaim political opinions, or to join in the discussions of party differences. Being so intelligent and well-informed, yet so unobtrusive, she was a charming companion. Able also to enter into the views of public men, and to quickly comprehend their plans, while appreciating every remark, she was not always looking out for the first lull in the conversation to express her own peculiar opinions, but on the contrary always listened intently and answered courteously. She was ever a good listener. Mr. Franklin Pierce, afterward President, at one time a boarder in the next house, was one of her most cordial and constant friends. At public assemblages he sometimes took charge of her, saying to her husband that he could go and talk politics with the gentlemen, and leave to him the more agreeable privilege of promenading and conversing with Mrs. Polk.

When, in 1839, they were bidding adieu to their friends, at the close of his Congressional service, Mrs. Seaton and Mrs. Gales were among the throng making the parting call. When Mrs. Seaton approached Mrs. Polk she said: "I am very sorry you are going away; we have had many pleasant hours together. But while I am sad on account of losing your society, there is a feeling of joyousness connected with it which I will not hide from you. When Mr. Polk is gone he will not be electioneering against Mr. Seaton, and will not record his vote against him." Messrs. Gales and Seaton were defeated in their efforts to obtain the public printing as long as Mr. Polk's influence was in Washington to oppose them; hence Mrs. Seaton's undisguised joy at his departure. "She was a perfect lady," added Mrs. Polk, in relating this incident, "and she would not have said that behind my back."

Among the pleasant episodes of this time of leave-taking, was the presentation of a poem in her honor by Judge Story. When Mr. Polk became Speaker of the House, he and his wife took a suite of rooms in a large house on Pennsylvania Avenue, known as Elliott's Building. It was not then considered proper for the Speaker to sit at table with the other members of Congress, the principal reason for this notion being the awkward positions which might ensue when the affairs and measures of Congress were discussed at meals, as would inevitably happen. The Speaker would be criticised or blamed, or at least often mentioned. The remainder of Elliott's Building was appropriated to the Supreme Court. Mrs. Polk frequently met the judges and members of the court, and became so well known to them that upon her departure many of them sent letters expressing regret at the loss of her presence. Judge McLean said in his letter that he "could not write poetry like Brother Story," but that his sentiments toward her were as warm, and his regrets at her leaving as great, as if he possessed the power to express himself in verse.

To Mrs. Polk,

On her leaving Washington.

Lady, I heard with saddened heart
　　The melancholy strain :
So soon from these fair scenes to part,
　　Ne'er to return again.

How swift have flown the busy hours,
　　Since we as strangers met ;
And some so bright, so strewed with flowers,
　　Are fresh in memory yet.

For I have listened to thy voice,
　　And watched thy playful mind,
Truth in its noblest sense thy choice,
　　Yet gentle, graceful, kind.

O, may thy future days be blest
　　With all our hearts approve ;
The sunshine of a spotless breast,
　　The joy of mutual love.

Farewell! And when thy distant home,
Cheered by thy smile shall be,
And o'er the past thick fancies come,
I ask one thought of me.

JOSEPH D. STORY.

WASHINGTON, February, 1839.

At the close of the session of Congress, March 4,
1839, the House passed a unanimous vote of thanks
to the retiring Speaker. In his farewell address, one
may plainly read between the lines his devotion to
duty, and the combination of firmly held opinions
with courteous deference to the opinions of those
opposed to him.

WIFE OF THE GOVERNOR.

CHAPTER V.

1839–1843.

REFRESHING indeed was the repose of the Columbia home to the two who returned to abide beneath its peaceful shelter, after fourteen years of going and coming, like birds of passage. This frequent change, and her light-hearted enjoyment of every day's experience, had been beneficial to mind and body, while the prospect of uninterrupted home life was all the sweeter, contrasted with the ceaseless change and variety of the last ten years and a half.

According to his habit Mr. Polk at once resumed the practice of law, his wife taking up the old daily routine, more than contented with her surroundings, securing order and peace by her presence, while sympathizing with her husband in all his studies and pursuits.

But this tranquillity was soon broken. Mr. Polk became a candidate for governor, and began the laborious task of canvassing the State. It was the most warmly contested campaign that had ever

taken place in Tennessee, and he went on horseback all over the State, making speeches everywhere to the crowds assembled to meet him.
His competitor was the then Governor, the Hon.
Newton Cannon. From the loopholes of her retreat at Columbia, his wife watched the conflict,
receiving frequent letters from her absent husband,
whose round of arduous labors had such an electric
effect in disturbing the quiet of her cottage-home.
At the election in August he was triumphant by a
majority of three or four thousand, a result highly
gratifying to General Jackson, who was delighted
to see his own Tennessee going in the political path
he considered safe and right.

Judge J. C. Guild relates the following incident
of that summer, which parts the curtains of the past
and affords a glimpse of the scenes and the persons
of more than half a century ago in Tennessee.

" After the August campaign of 1839, which
resulted in the election of James K. Polk to the
gubernatorial chair, the leading Democratic politi-
·cians in and about Nashville assembled with their
families and a concourse of young people at Tyree
Springs, in Sumner County, for a little rest and
recreation.

" General Jackson was there. Felix Grundy, then
Attorney-General of Mr. Van Buren's administra-

tion, with Judge Campbell, the old minister to Russia, General Armstrong, a lineal descendant of the gallant old trooper, and captain of General Jackson's body-guard in the Creek war, Governor Polk, who had just been elected, and all the old notables of that party, with a bevy of beautiful young ladies to grace the occasion, were also there.

"The weather was delightful, the spring waters refreshing, and arrangements were made to pass the time pleasantly. An old gardener, not far distant, was employed to bring fresh melons, fruits and flowers to the party every morning, and upon the greensward under the ample shade of the great elms with which the yard was studded, was held every day, after breakfast, a moot or mock court, of which Judge Grundy was the Chief Justice, and General Jackson, who sat near by, an associate. The court was opened in due form every morning by Colonel Harris, the Marshal, and the young gentlemen, indicted for every little trivial offence conceivable, such as failing to bow when passing a lady, or any other slight breach of common courtesy, were brought up for trial. To be tried was to be fined. No one got clear. Judge Grundy announced that one rule of the court was that he who grumbled at the magnitude of his fine should be fined double.　So the fines were always paid without a murmur, and the party was constantly supplied with watermelons, muskmelons, canta- loupes, peaches and pears in abundance, while all the ladies had a daily supply of beautiful flowers.

" After each and every gentleman had been fined several times, the marshal reported to the court that the expenses were becoming a little too bind- ing on some of the guests, and asked what should be done.　On ascertaining that the wagon had arrived that morning and was full of nice supplies, Judge Grundy decided that as so much money had been already paid to the gardener, his prices must be exceedingly high, and therefore he should be indicted at once, and brought before the court for extortion.　Accordingly, the old gardener, who had been a soldier with General Jackson in the Creek War or at New Orleans, was formally in- dicted and brought into court.　He had retained two eminent lawyers of Louisiana, who happened to be of the party, as his counsel, and they argued the case with much ingenuity and humor for an hour or more, taking the ground that not being of the party, their client was not within the juris- diction of the court.　To the guests who attentively followed and enjoyed the argument, it seemed that the old gardener would certainly get clear, but at the close, Judge Grundy turned to General Jackson and asked, ' General, is not a sutler subject to the rules and regulations of the camp? '

" General Jackson replied, 'Most certainly, Judge Grundy.'

" ' Oh ! ' exclaimed the old gardener, 'it is all over with me; there is no appeal from the decision of General Jackson.'

" So the Judge fined him the entire load of his wagon, which he promptly delivered without a word of complaint; albeit a subscription was quietly taken up, and the old gardener was fully remunerated.

" And it was quite remarkable that during that week so pleasantly spent there, not a word of politics or upon any question of public affairs was heard, notwithstanding it was a sort of Democratic love-feast."

The capital of Tennessee continued many years at Knoxville, where it had first been established; then it was removed to Kingston, then to Murfrees-borough, and finally, in 1827, to Nashville. This city had never enjoyed the luxury of a governor's mansion, and the new incumbent rented the large dwelling on Cherry Street known as the Craighead house. The rent, only five hundred dollars a year, shows the difference between those times and the

present.   The Governor's yearly salary was two
thousand dollars.   Cherry Street was then a choice
neighborhood, and Mrs. Polk had sunny memories
of the excellent society of those early days.   Across
the street was the home of Col. Samuel D. Morgan,
an active leader in the Whig party.   This, however,
did not prevent genuine friendliness between his
family and the Governor and his wife, who were
often invited over to dine with other guests.   These
invitations Mr. Polk generally declined, saying he
"could not lose half a day just to go and dine."
But he wished his wife to go, and she usually represented him on these occasions.   The attachment of
the members of Colonel Morgan's family to her
sometimes produced a division of sentiment in the
household.   One evening Colonel Morgan had an
illumination in honor of some Whig event, — perhaps the triumph of the Whig party in the hotly
waged presidential campaign of 1840, — when one
of his daughters followed him as he lighted the
candles in the window-panes, and blew them out.
He bore this outbreak of opposition patiently for
a little while, relighting the candles; but suddenly
turning round, he said, "That is enough now!
Just come and help me to light these candles!"
And she was compelled to assist him in the display so obnoxious to her friend across the street.

Colonel Morgan was one of the Board of Commissioners intrusted with the charge of building the State House. During the Civil War, earthworks were thrown up around this building by the Federal army, to form a fortification, which obstructed the view from the lower terrace. The sides of the hill were stony and rough, in strange contrast to the noble temple of liberty rising above them. That sight is entirely forgotten now in the beautiful grounds surrounding the Capitol. The expanses of luxuriant grass, the growing trees, the walks winding up and around the hill, with frequent flights of steps to aid in the ascent, the fountain and flowers, and the equestrian statue seem to make Jackson, Tennessee's beloved hero, the perpetual guardian of his adopted home. The crown of this little gem of a park is the fine view, taking in at one sweep the city below with its church-spires, its vistas of streets, its public buildings and happy homes embowered in trees; and the green country beyond; miles and miles of as delightsome a land as was ever bestowed upon man by the bountiful hand of the Creator. This extensive landscape has the magical effect of making the Capitol grounds seem larger than they really are, imparting the sense of elevation and of ample space.

Not far from Colonel Morgan's residence lived

James Walker, the father of William Walker, of
Nicaragua fame. His wife was a sister of Caleb C.
Norvell, editor of the "Nashville Whig," whose
vigorous editorials against Mr. Polk and his party
were issued with telling effect every other day.
Mrs. Walker who was warmly attached to Mrs.
Polk, was so aggrieved at Mr. Norvell's onslaughts
upon the husband of her friend, that she would
sometimes say to her, "I haven't opened my
brother's paper to-day, for I dislike so much to
read what he says against your husband." When
party spirit was heated and ready to burst into flame
at the slightest touch of antagonism, the Governor
would say to his wife, "When you hear that so-
and-so, and you will hear it, is going to vote against
me, don't you get excited and say, 'I never will
forgive him.'" He thought that every man had
a right to his own opinion, and so far from being offended with those opposed to him, he was
always ready, as his wife said, "to give them the
hand."

Opposite to Mr. Walker lived Col. Thomas
Claiborne, whose son, young Tom Claiborne, was
Mr. Polk's companion during his canvass for the
governorship, keeping his papers and pamphlets,
and taking charge of the documents after every
day's speaking. Another neighbor was Dr. Felix

Robertson, noted for being the first white male child born in Nashville. His father, in the spring of 1780, founded in these Indian-haunted wilds the little settlement of " Nashborough," and the name " Felix," given to the new settler shows that they were happy in their adopted home.

Near the close of Governor Polk's term, in 1841, he gave " a party " to the General Assembly of Tennessee, which in those days was considered a suitable precursor to the termination of his governorship. One of the expected guests was the Ex-President living then in his chosen retirement, the Hermitage. On account of ill-health, he was unable to be present. Mrs. Polk's escort to the table on that occasion was the Rev. R. B. C. Howell.

Governor Polk was a candidate for re-election, but was defeated by Mr. James C. Jones, and once more Mrs. Polk had the pleasing prospect of living in Columbia. Gifted with a keen appreciation of social life, she nevertheless appreciated as keenly the pleasures of a home, though narrower, still sweeter and deeper. This endowment of opposite qualities made her free from the limitations of circumstances, and capable of happiness and usefulness wherever she might be. She said sometimes that she would go into her husband's study and finding him engaged as usual, would say, " You work so much." Taking up a newspaper, he would quietly reply, " Sarah, here is something I wish you to read." " And so he set me to work too." In giving him sympathy and assistance in many wifely ways, she found no time for loneliness. A letter often came with the request, " Can't you come to Nashville? I want to confer with you." In the evening he would ask, " Sarah, would n't you like to go to Nashville? " Mrs. Polk laughingly said, in telling this, " I cannot find fault now with the ladies for going away from home so much, because I went so often with Mr. Polk. I always went, except in cases when it was obviously unsuitable, and then it would have been foolish to go. He always wished me to go, and he would say, 'Why should you stay at home? To take care of the house? Why, if the house burns down, we can live without it.' "

She sometimes went with him to the plantation in Mississippi, going in a carriage and taking a riding-horse, that he might change to horseback whenever he so desired. They were entertained in the overseer's house and there received the visits of the neighbors. He was very kind to the negroes on his plantation and careful of their comfort.

His delicate constitution, weakened by unremitting labor, required the rest which could be had only by adequate sleep. The presence of his wife often prevented an indulgence in late hours, to which he was exposed by those who came to talk with him on law matters or political affairs. To help him in this way was one strong motive impelling her frequent journeying with him.

In April, 1842, they had the pleasure of a visit from Ex-President Martin Van Buren, who was the occupant of the White House when they left Washington in 1839. He was accompanied by the Hon. James K. Paulding of New York, his Secretary of the Navy. They had visited Jackson at the Hermitage, and after spending a few days with them, went to Lexington, to see Mr. Clay. Old Hickory and Young Hickory gave every attention to their distinguished guests.

The calm of this domestic life was again disturbed by Mr. Polk's canvass for the governorship in 1843. Letters frequently passed between them in the long absences occasioned by these canvasses. Writing from Jackson, West Tennessee, April 4, he says, " Yesterday I addressed a very large crowd, including the leading men of both parties from every part of the State. I spoke for three and a half hours. I received your letter to-

day. I will be at Savannah on the 14th, at which
time I hope to receive another letter from you.
After that, the points on the main stage-route
where letters will reach me without delay are
Somerville, Memphis, and Camden, and I shall
hope to hear from you at each of those places.
If any letters come which you think important,
enclose them to me."

On the 18th of June he was a guest of Dr.
J. G. M. Ramsey, at Mecklenburg, four miles
from Knoxville, at the romantic spot where the
Holston and the French Broad rivers unite. From
there he wrote, " You write a little despondingly,
and it distresses me that you seem to be in low
spirits. If I could be with you, you know I would.
It is, however, impossible for the next six weeks,
and I hope you will endeavor to renew your former
cheerfulness and good spirits." It was his custom
in every letter to her who was so practically his
help-meet, to begin with the words, " My dear
Wife," a short, simple phrase, but rich and weighty
with meaning.

Mr. Jones the opposition candidate, was re-
elected and Mr. Polk returned home. In addition to his law practice, he carried on a large
correspondence with political friends, among whom
were Silas Wright of New York, and all the Demo-

cratic leaders of that day. The interchange of letters between him and General Jackson was frequent. It is said that Jackson was one of the most indefatigable letter-writers in the whole country.

WIFE OF THE PRESIDENT.

CHAPTER VI.

1844–1845.

IN May, 1844, came the stirring event of Mr.
Polk's nomination to the presidency by the
Democratic National Convention at Baltimore. This
was followed by a season of conflict and of inevitable suspense and anxiety; but those weeks of
weary waiting were afterward suffused with the lustre of a triumphant ending, and whatever sadness
there might have been was forgotten in the joy
that followed. In November, by a majority of
sixty-five electoral votes, and of about forty thousand in the popular suffrage, Mr. Polk was chosen
President of the United States.

In those days all news travelled by mail, then the
quickest mode of conveyance. Returns had been
received from a number of States sufficient to show
that the vote of New York would decide the combat
between the Whig and Democratic parties, — between Mr. Clay and Mr. Polk. It was generally
believed that New York would vote for Mr. Clay,

and the Whig papers were constantly declaring that
he was elected.   The news from New York was slow
in coming in, owing to the magnitude of the territory and the closeness of the contest.   But, at his
home in Columbia, Mr. Polk knew of his election
twenty hours before the people of that town knew
it, and fifteen hours before it was known by the
people of Nashville.   The welcome information
was sent to him by Gen. Robert Armstrong, a
warm friend, who was the postmaster at Nashville.

The daily Eastern mail arrived about 9 o'clock at
night, and General Armstrong was in the habit of
opening the packages from all the principal cities of
the country, and comparing the number of letters
with the way-bill.   In opening the package from
Cincinnati he saw, in pencil, written on the way-bill
by the postmaster there, that New York had certainly gone for Polk and Dallas.   The Nashville
postmaster quietly placed the writing in his pocket,
handed the letters to one of his clerks for distribu-
tion, and retired to his private room.   He immediately sent a servant to Mr. George L. Sloan, pro-
prietor of a large livery establishment, a devoted
Democrat, and an active partisan.   He was asked if
he could reach Columbia, with an important letter
for Governor Polk, by daylight next morning.   He
said he could, and while he went to his stable for a

fast horse, General Armstrong wrote a brief letter to Mr. Polk, telling him of the news from the post-master at Cincinnati. Mr. Sloan rode rapidly, and obtaining a fresh horse from a friend a few miles beyond Franklin, reached Columbia, a distance of forty miles, by early dawn. Mr. Polk was called from his bed-chamber, and Mr. Sloan delivered the letter in person, not knowing its contents. He then quietly left the town, and leisurely came home, taking his own horse on the way.

Mr. Polk was very much gratified, of course, and told his wife the exciting news. They agreed to keep it quiet, and went about their daily duties as usual. During the day political opponents, calling at his office, or meeting him on the street, would say, " Well, Governor, we are sorry that you are defeated, but glad Mr. Clay is elected." Mr. Polk thanked these personal friends for their good wishes, knowing however that they were mistaken. The mail next morning announced that the large elec-toral vote of New York had been cast for Mr. Polk, and that he was elected.

A public meeting of the Democrats of Columbia and of Maury County was soon called, and the joy of the Democrats knew no bounds. Crowds came pouring into town, the houses were illuminated, and Mr. Polk's house was besieged by a multitude who

came with a band of music, and with noisy hurrahs
and other manifestations of pleasure usual on such
occasions.

Mrs. Polk was in the parlor with congratulating
lady visitors, when a gentleman entered, saying,
" Mrs. Polk, some of your husband's friends wish to
come into the house, but we will not let the crowd
in, because the street is muddy and your carpets
and furniture will be spoiled."

" The house is thrown open to everybody," was
the reply.   " Let them all come in; they will not
hurt the carpets."

This decision was exactly in accord with Mr.
Polk's wishes and preferences, if not in great part
unconsciously impelled by them; and coming in
that moment, he heartily seconded the enthusiastic
invitation. The next day, the hospitable lady sent
word to the gentleman who was so politely careful
regarding the soiling of her furniture that, just as
she expected, the crowd "left no marks except
marks of respect."

The Whigs were in deep sorrow, and Mr. Clay's
defeat was greatly deplored by his large and influ-
ential party.   He was their idol, and probably no
politician ever had warmer friends or more bitter
enemies, General Jackson alone excepted.   Large
sums of money had been wagered, and changed

hands, on the result. In Tennessee, owing to the presence of General Jackson, the struggle was especially violent. Every effort possible was put forth on both sides to obtain even a single vote, and bets were freely made that Tennessee would go for Mr. Clay. The race was close, and Mr. Polk lost Tennessee by only one hundred and thirteen votes in the entire State.

Mr. Polk visited Nashville, and was honored with a public reception in which both parties joined. A civic and military procession escorted him to the Court House, where he was addressed by the Hon. A. O. P. Nicholson. In the evening many buildings were illuminated, and joy and hilarity prevailed.

One day, at Columbia, in these agitating times, a lady remarked to a friend of Mrs. Polk's that she hoped Mr. Clay would be elected to the presidency, because his wife was a good housekeeper, and made fine butter. To this singular remark, which seemed to cast a reflection upon the wife of Mr. Clay's opponent, a rather spirited retort was made, and a wordy little passage at arms followed, which was duly reported to the lady supposed to be most interested as the rival of Mrs. Clay. She was amused at the incident, and said to her friend, " Now, Ophelia, you go to-morrow morning and tell Mrs. Blank that you are sorry for all those sharp

replies you made, and tell her I said that if I should
be so fortunate as to reach the White House, I
expect to live on twenty-five thousand dollars
a year, and I will neither keep house nor make
butter. This answer will not offend her, and neither
will I be offended." This pacific message had the
desired effect. There has perhaps been no other instance in which a capacity to make good butter was
considered a fitting excellence for the President's
wife.

In February, 1845, the journey to Washington
was begun, Mr. and Mrs. Polk first going to the
Hermitage, near Nashville, to see General Jackson.
Mr. Jenkins says, " The leave-taking was affectionate and impressive, for each felt conscious that
in all probability it was a farewell forever. Ere
another harvest moon shed its holy light upon a
spot hallowed by so many memories and associations, the ' hero of New Orleans ' and ' defender
of the Constitution ' slept that sleep which knows
no waking. A few years passed, and he to whom
that parting blessing had been given with so fair
and bright a promise of a long life before him, had
also joined the assembly of the dead. Truly, the
realities of history are sometimes stranger far than
the wildest creations of fiction."

Among those who accompanied Mr. and Mrs.

Polk was Mr. V. K. Stevenson. They went from Nashville to Wheeling on a small new steamer built of cedar, called by the river men the " cedar boat." In going up the Ohio, some distance below Louisville, in a terrific storm, the boat was blown ashore and among the trees. Colonel Stevenson says that amid the general dismay Mr. and Mrs. Polk did not seem in the least alarmed. When they passed Louisville it was late at night, yet many people were at the wharf, sending up cheer after cheer.

On Sunday a band of music came on board, intending to honor the President's party by playing during the day. When Mrs. Polk first heard the music, impelled by her sense of right and propriety, she requested Mr. Stevenson to have it stopped, because it was unseemly on that day. He said, " Madame, it can be done." When the matter reached Mr. Polk's ears he quietly remarked, " Sarah directs all domestic affairs, and she thinks that is domestic."

At Madison, Indiana, a large party came aboard and warmly welcomed the passenger toward whom all eyes were turning in hope and anxious expectation. Mr. Stevenson presented many persons separately, and toward the close of the ceremony he introduced a noted, old-time Irish school-teacher, who, standing in front of Mr. Polk, bowed low and

6

said, " Yure koontenance is indicative of a bro–a–d
ba—sis," spinning out the latter words to their
fullest extent. Then going behind him and bowing again, he repeated the same words. Passing
to the front, he again went through the whimsical
solemnity, and left the boat perfectly satisfied that
he had made known the true character of the new
chief executive.

At Cincinnati, as at all other landings, crowds
were on the shore, and in every case, Mr. Stevenson presented Mr. Polk, who made a brief reply
of thanks. During their stay of a day or two in
Wheeling, there were throngs of callers, among
whom were representatives of all classes, and one
lady felt herself obliged to apologize because so
many of the " common people" were there. That
act of " politeness" only showed that she had failed
to understand the character of this woman, whose
exaltation, so far from raising a barrier between her
and the masses of the people, had enabled her the
better to discover the good in them, and to appreciate their kindness. Mrs. Polk in the retrospect
of her life, called herself a " proud woman," and
such she was, in the highest sense, — proud of her
husband, of his worth and his success; proud of
the position and happiness with which she had been
endowed; and too proud to hold herself aloof from

the humblest person. She had no fear of any possible tarnish by such association, and was affable and gracious to all.

From Wheeling to Cumberland, they travelled by carriage over the National Road. This highway was built from Wheeling to Baltimore, for the purpose of transporting government troops and stores over the mountains. The most important consideration, however, was the inducement it would offer emigrants to settle the western lands, and thus bring these lands into market for sale. For years this project provoked fierce discussions in Congress, Mr. Polk being opposed to it, while Mr. Clay advocated the measure. Once an object of great public interest, and a means of comparative ease in travel, the National Road is now scarcely more than a memory, and flourishes only in the encyclopædia.

At Cumberland, they took the railroad train, and at the Relay House, near Baltimore, were met by committees from Washington, Baltimore, and other places. Here they were also joined by the Vice-President-elect, the Hon. George M. Dallas. Mrs. Polk said that "he was an elegant man, tall, exceedingly handsome, and gentle in manner." Here a scene occurred, quite out of keeping with the dignity of the occasion, and illustrating the heterogeneous mixture of affairs, the continual nearness

of right and wrong, of high and low. A pickpocket
in the crowd had doubtless heard that Mr. Stevenson
paid all the expenses of the trip for Mr. Polk, and
he accordingly undertook to get into his pocket.
He had discovered that there were no outside
pockets, and was in the act of reaching over and
trying to get his hand into the inside breast pocket,
when Mr. Stevenson caught it, and by twisting his
arm forced him to come round in front. The fel-
low was an affrighted, woe-begone spectacle, and
when it was learned that he had failed in his lawless
purpose, was released.

They reached Washington about two weeks before the 4th of March, and in this interim Mr.
Polk accomplished the delicate task of selecting
the officers of his Cabinet. The usages of society
had established relations of close intercourse between the household of the President and those
of the Cabinet officers, and his selection of these
exerted an influence on his home life as well as
on public affairs. To the office of Secretary of
State he appointed James Buchanan, of Pennsylvania, whose long service in the Senate ad-
mirably fitted him for that high position. The
Treasury Department was committed to the care
of Robert J. Walker, of Mississippi. The War
Department was placed under the charge of ex-

Governor William L. Marcy, of New York, and
the success of his conduct in the struggle with
Mexico proved the wisdom of Mr. Polk's choice.
George Bancroft, of Massachusetts, was made Secretary of the Navy; but after a short time he was sent
to the Court of St. James, and John Y. Mason,
of Virginia, appointed in his stead. The office of
Postmaster-General was given to Cave Johnson,
of Tennessee, and during his occupancy of that
position the reduction of the rates of postage was
begun. John Y. Mason had been appointed Attorney-General, but upon his becoming Secretary of the
Navy, Nathan Clifford, of Maine, was selected in
his place. Mr. Clifford was afterward sent as a
commissioner to Mexico, and Isaac Toucey, of Connecticut, became Attorney-General. For the confi-
dential post of Private Secretary, the President
chose one of his nephews, J. Knox Walker.

The 4th of March was rainy and cheerless, but
the ceremonies of the day filled the streets with
gayly dressed people. According to custom, the
President-elect was accompanied by the retiring
President, and they rode to the capitol in an open
carriage drawn by four horses, and escorted by
the chief marshal and his aids, who carried as
emblems of the new head of the republic, bâtons
of young hickory, decked with a profusion of

ribbons. The President-elect and his escort were
received in the Senate Chamber by the assembled
Congress. Mrs. Polk, with several of her special
friends, witnessed the proceedings from the gallery.
When the oath of office had been taken by Mr.
Dallas, and some other formalities had been completed, Mr. Polk was escorted to the eastern
portico by the members of Congress, the foreign
legations, and other distinguished persons. This
procession was led, as was customary, by the
judges of the Supreme Court, attired in their
robes of office, seeming thus to give judicial sanc-
tion to the choice of the people. The vicinity
of the capitol was crowded with enthusiastic spectators. Mrs. Polk with her friends was seated on
the portico. She held in her hand what may be
called a national fan, which had been presented
to her. In the folds, above an ivory handle of
beautiful open-work, were eleven circles enclosing
the portraits of the eleven Presidents, from Washington to Polk, each inscribed with the name and
the date of the term of office. Above Mr. Polk's
was written, "President-elect." In the flower-
gilded spaces between these circles were the United
States escutcheon, and statues of the Goddess of
Liberty. On the reverse was an oval picture of
the signing of the Declaration of Independence.

THE INAUGURATION FAN.

Chief-Justice Taney administered the oath of office. The multitude listened quietly during the delivery of the Inaugural Address, then with shouts and cheers applauding the new-made President, joined the procession, and attended him in a vast body to the door of the White House.

The Bible upon which the oath was taken is a small one, printed in clear, minion type, bound in black morocco, and was presented to Mrs. Polk by Alexander Hunter, chief marshal of the District of Columbia. On the fly-leaves he wrote the following letter: —

"MADAME, — I feel it alike an honor, a pleasure, and a duty, to present you (as I now do) the sacred volume on which the oath of office as President of these United States was administered to your honored husband on the 4th day of March just passed. I will not permit myself to doubt that it will be esteemed and preserved by you as a sacred and not unbefitting memorial of an event of interest to your family. It is calculated to unite in solemn associations the recollection of the highest honor on this earth, with the bright hopes and glorious promises of another and happier sphere of existence. United with your distinguished husband in the enjoyment of the utmost favor of his countrymen, and the

highest station which their votes and their confidence can bestow, when time shall have passed,
and the troubles and the honors of this life shall
have known their termination, may your union
still continue undisturbed, and be blessed with
that happiness which the Holy Book teaches, as
the hope and the promise."

A group of select friends dined with the President
and his wife at the White House, and this eventful
day was closed with the customary Inauguration
Ball. This took place in Carusi's Hall, and was intended as an opportunity for the people to get a
near view of the new chief magistrate. To prevent
too great a crowd, the tickets were sold at ten dollars
each. When the President and his party entered
and took their places on a platform at the end of
the hall, the dancing ceased, and the band played
" Hail to the Chief," and there was a general reception. Mrs. Polk remembered that she wore a ma-
zarine blue velvet dress, with a deeply fringed cape.
When the ceremony of introduction and handshak-
ing was over, Mr. and Mrs. Polk with their friends
left the hall.

The new mistress of the White House showed
her simplicity and moderation in her decision concerning the renovation customary with each new
resident in the old mansion. The " New York

Journal of Commerce" commended her sensible views as follows: —

" A couple of upholsterers who went from this city to procure so much of the job as falls within their department, came back with very reduced expectations. They were referred to the President's lady, who gave them a courteous interview of three quarters of an hour, but told them that only the public rooms would require repairs, for if the private apartments had been satisfactory to Mrs. Tyler, they would be so to herself."

One day, soon after the beginning of the administration, some one sent a fine riding-horse to the White House stable. When the President heard of the gift, he told his secretary to have the horse sent to the livery-stable and to inform the owner where it was. He would accept presents of little worth, such as books, canes, etc , but must decline any of larger value. This wise course effectually closed an opening to irregularities and corruption. Not long afterward, the citizens of New York wished to present to him a carriage and horses, but he declined the proffered kindness. These two instances convinced the public of his determination, and no one afterward ventured to offer a costly gift, for fear of giving offence. Sometimes a naval officer would say to Mrs. Polk that in a foreign country he had seen some rare or rich article which he wished very much to bring home to her, but had feared to do so. In later life she said that she did not then realize as fully as afterward, the worth of such a rigid and self-denying uprightness, and would smilingly say to her husband, " Oh, I have lost so many pretty things by your refusing to take costly presents ! " He would never consent to accept such favors for his wife any more than for himself.

Mr. Polk had been privately informed that the Hon. John C. Calhoun, the Secretary of State in Mr. Tyler's Cabinet, was desirous of remaining in that office until the annexation of Texas was consummated, a measure which he ardently advocated. Mr. Polk was also solicitous concerning it, and Mr. Calhoun naturally expected to remain. But the pressure of the politicians was against his retention, and Mr. Polk tendered him the mission to England. This post was declined, and preparations were made for his return to South Carolina. He had for years cherished a cordial friendship for Mrs. Polk, and calling to bid her farewell, she expressed her regret that he had decided not to accept the mission. " Madame," replied the distinguished South Carolinian, " you know me well enough to be aware that I am a domestic man in my nature and habits, and that such a place would not suit my taste." She admired his great powers, and his honest adherence to the political principles he believed to be right, whatever might be the convictions of others. He was a worthy descendant of the resolute Huguenots, many of whom in their expatriation fled to South Carolina, and enriched that State by their noble character and valuable labors.

The ladies of the diplomatic circle added much to the vivacity and enjoyment of social affairs. The wife of the Russian Minister possessed unusual attractions. Mrs. Polk had known Madame Bodisco when she was Miss Williams, and a pupil at the Georgetown school. It is said that the dignified ambassador then met the young school-girl who subsequently became his bride.

Of those connected with the families of the secretaries, perhaps it was to Mrs. Marcy that the President's wife was most strongly attached. They often went to church together, Mrs. Marcy attending the Presbyterian, with her friend, and Mrs. Polk returning the favor by going with Mrs. Marcy to the Baptist Church. During the fourteen years of her residence in Washington, while her husband was in Congress, Mrs. Polk was a regular attendant of the First Presbyterian Church on Four-and-a-half Street, not far from the capitol. When she returned, it was supposed that she would worship with the Rev. Mr. Lowrie's church, not far from the White

House. But she continued to frequent the old sanctuary, though it was a mile away. "I loved the familiar place," she said; "and why should I not go there, when it was my intention to ride, and a mile more would make no difference?"

The dazzling and deceptive allurements inseparable from high position had no power to blind her to the truth. She regularly attended church, duly observed the Sabbath, and maintained Christian charities. "The greater the prosperity," she said, "the deeper the sense of gratitude to the Almighty Power from whom all blessings flow. My heart never yielded to worldly honors or self-vanity." In her new home, one effect of her principles was the discontinuance of dancing. This stroke of authority made a sensation, and with a few exceptions was universally applauded. Some young ladies remonstrated: "Oh, Mrs. Polk, why will you not let us dance? These rooms are so magnificent." "Would you dance in so public a place as this?" she would ask; and when they said yes her reply was, "I would not. To dance in these rooms would be undignified, and it would be respectful neither to the house nor to the office. How indecorous it would seem for dancing to be going on in one apartment, while in another we were conversing with dignitaries of the republic or

ministers of the gospel. This unseemly juxtaposi-
tion would be likely to occur at any time, were
such amusements permitted."

The "Nashville Union" thus applauded her
decision: —

" The example of Mrs. Polk can hardly fail of exerting
a salutary influence. Especially does it rebuke the conduct of those ladies who professing godliness, nevertheless
dishonor its profession by their eager participation in the
follies and amusements of the world. However politicians
may differ in regard to the merit of Mr. Polk's administration,
there can be no difference as respects that of his lady, in
her department of the Presidential mansion."

Mrs. Polk saw Mrs. Madison frequently, and enjoyed taking her for a drive on pleasant summer
afternoons. It was the custom to invite her to
every Cabinet dinner, and to all entertainments
given at the White House, the President himself
escorting her to the table. She was always attired
in black silk or velvet, with a kerchief of muslin
and lace around her neck and shoulders, folded
across the bosom. In after years Mrs. Polk
wrote, "The White House was the abode of
pleasure while I was there." At the weekly receptions, she pleased every caller with her words
of welcome. At the large dinners, complimentary
to distinguished persons, members of the Cabinet,

civil, military, and naval officers, eminent citizens, diplomatists, and noted foreigners, the dignity and courtesy of the hostess impressed every one, and her praises were trumpeted by the newspapers.

The President's duties left him little time for even a cursory scanning of the numerous newspapers. There were frequent allusions to his administration, and it was necessary for him to know the drift of public feeling and opinion. He would send the papers to his wife, requesting her to examine them and mark such articles as it was desirable for him to read. This task, requiring judgment and knowledge of public affairs, she gladly performed. Carefully folding the papers with the marked pieces outside, where a glance might detect them, she would place the pile beside his chair, so that whenever a few moments of leisure came, he could find and read without loss of time. Knowing much of political affairs she found pleasure in the society of gentlemen; and some one remarked that " she was always in the parlor with Mr. Polk."

In a letter to her from Judge Catron, dated at Nashville, June, 1845, he says : —

" We had the pleasure to hear by Mrs. Marshall's letter that you were very well, and the President not — overworked, of course. On this head I am uneasy, and advise *lectures* on your part, on all inordinate and especially irregular labors. The machinery of government looks well at a distance, smooth, still, and statesmanlike. I think the President has deeply impressed upon him the early copy set him in the old field school: ' Least said is soonest mended.' It is worth more in practice than all ever written in Italy and France on slippery policy. All sides seem to vie in vaunting you, and if this keeps on through the four years, will stilt you up to so giddy a height that you may incur more danger in getting down than in climbing up."

The following paper, written by Mr. Polk on his fiftieth birthday, Sunday, November 2, 1845, was found among his manuscripts, long afterward:

" Attended the Methodist Church (called the Foundery Church) to-day, in company with my private secretary, J. Knox Walker. It was an inclement day, there being rain from an early hour in the morning, and Mrs. Polk and the ladies of my household did not attend church to-day. Mrs. Polk being a member of the Presbyterian Church, I generally attend that church with her, though my opinions and predilections are in favor of the Methodist Church. This was my birthday, being fifty years old. The text was from the Acts of the Apostles, chap. 17, verse 31: ' Because He hath appointed a day, in the which He will judge the world in righteousness by that man whom He hath ordained.' It was communion day, and the sermon was solemn and forcible. It awakened the reflection that I had lived fifty years, and that before fifty years more would expire I would be sleeping with the generations which have gone before me. I thought of the vanity of this world's honors, how little they would profit me half a century hence, and that it was time for me to be ' putting my house in order.' "

A New York newspaper of the time says of him:

" He would have a pew in church and regularly occupy it. No visitor would be admitted into his house on the Sabbath except family acquaintances. If a week's journey was to be undertaken he would start on Monday morning and reach the place on Saturday night. And all this though not a professor of religion. Mr. Polk had a delicacy and propriety of feeling, which showed how well and kindly he had yielded his heart and his habits to a most auspicious domestic influence ; how fully he acknowledged the legitimate influence of a pious wife, to whom he was bound by ties of the strongest affection, and who indeed was, in many senses, his guardian angel amid the perils and darkness of the way."

LIFE AT THE WHITE HOUSE.

THE PRESIDENT AND MRS. POLK.

From a copy of one of the first Daguerreotypes made at Washington, 1847 or 1848.

CHAPTER VII.

1846–1849.

ONE afternoon in July, when the beams of the sun were flaming with scorching heat, Mrs. Polk was sitting at a window overlooking a part of the White House grounds where several men were at work. Her husband was absorbed in writing, and there was no one else present.

"Mr. Polk," she suddenly said, "the writers of the Declaration of Independence were mistaken when they affirmed that all men are created equal."

"Oh, Sarah," said he, "that is one of your foolish fancies."

"But, Mr. Polk," she returned, "let me illustrate what I mean. There are those men toiling in the heat of the sun, while you are writing, and I am sitting here fanning myself, in this house as airy and delightful as a palace, surrounded with every comfort. Those men did not choose such a lot in life, neither did we ask for ours; we were created for these places."

Mr. Polk was amused at her criticism on the venerable and honored document, and rehearsed the incident as an example of " Sarah's acumen." Circumstances certainly seem sometimes to disprove the grand truth that all men are created with equal rights to life, liberty, and the pursuit of happiness; but she believed, as we all do, that it is nevertheless the powerful principle underlying the beneficent liberty and marvellous growth of our country. It is the wonder-working Aladdin's lamp of the Occident, holding forth the radiant light of a new era, and its mighty genius is building homes of peace and content for the poor and oppressed of every land.

The following extract is from a letter of Judge Lewis of Lancaster, Pennsylvania, who was Mrs. Polk's agent in the following incident: —

"On the 4th of July, 1846, the President's mansion was thrown open for the reception of visitors, and the rooms gradually filled with guests 'of high and low degree.' Amid the motley groups present, the President's lady was receiving with becoming courtesy the guests who advanced to pay their respects, when she perceived an old man, supported by a long cane, and dressed in humble garb, totter into the room, and in a diffident manner take a station at a distance and gaze with

unmingled wonder upon the scene before him.
Mrs. Polk despatched a gentleman with whom
she was then conversing, to bring the old man
to her, and talked with him for some time with
the kindly sympathy for old age which is a beautiful feature of woman's character. He said that
he was one hundred and five years old, had dined
with Washington, and his memory reached thirty
years beyond the stirring events of the American
Revolution. His reminiscences of bygone times
were received with attention by his auditress, and
when other guests claimed her ear, she followed
the old man with her eye, and directed that the
venerable visitor should be treated with special
respect. This incident, while it evinces that Mrs.
Polk's heart was where it always is, in the right
place, speaks volumes in favor of our republican
institutions. The poor man enters the Palace of
the People, stands in the presence of assembled
senators and ambassadors, converses with the lofti-
est lady in the republic, and receives every attention
and respect."

In those times, there were few of the flowers and
vines whose natural grace now adorns the grounds
of the White House. Some years later, funds were
voted by Congress for the establishment and main-
tenance of a greenhouse there. A conservatory

was attached to the Patent Office, but the public did not have the privilege of plucking the flowers. Whenever the President's wife came, the gardener cut a profusion of blossoms, and arranging them into a handsome bouquet, presented it to her. Occasionally, visitors who observed this would ask a similar favor, to which his reply would be that he was not allowed to give the flowers away. When it was rejoined, " You gave some to that lady," he would disclose that lady's name. Some of them would be satisfied, but others were offended. " I did not desire this distinction to be made between others and myself," she said, " and I requested the gardener not to cut any more flowers for me. His reply was, ' Madame, if you will receive them, I will still give you flowers.' But I did not wish for the attention. I always had so much that I could not wish for more."

A letter from Washington in November, 1846, says : —

" At no period in our history have we seen the hospitalities of the White House more handsomely dispensed, or displayed with greater republican simplicity. There is no extra formality exhibited when a Secretary or some other high officer of government presents himself. The quiet, unheralded citizen receives a polite and cordial salutation, as well as the rich man or the Minister of State. I was struck with Mrs. Polk's patriotic sentiments. A gallant lieutenant, just from the bloody but glorious conflict at Monterey was there also; and as she carried back his thoughts to the distant field of his fame, he caught the inspiration, and dwelt briefly upon some of the thrilling incidents of those scenes. In the course of this animated conversation, the young officer remarked that something — I do not now recollect what — was rather too democratic; to which Mrs. Polk replied that whatever sustained the honor and advanced the interests of the country, whether regarded as democratic or not, she admired and applauded."

On Christmas Day Mr. Polk's thoughts were with his old home in Columbia, and with the central figure of that home, his mother, to whom he wrote as follows: —

"DEAR MOTHER: — It has been many months since I have written to you, but you have been constantly in my affectionate remembrance. My whole time has been occupied in the performance of my public duties. This is Christmas Day, and is one of the most quiet days I have spent since I have been President. Congress does not sit, the public offices are all closed, and the population generally attend church. My official term has nearly half expired. My public responsibilities and cares are very great, and I shall rejoice when the period shall arrive when I can bid adieu to public life forever. I shall return to Tennessee at the close of my term, and spend the remainder of my life in quiet retirement."

In the summer of 1847 the President, with several state officers and a few personal friends, made a tour in the northern and eastern States. A Buffalo newspaper had a long article about the reception in that city, and said, among many other good things: —

" We are not in the least addicted to man-worship ; we look upon the man with no more regard because he holds an office, for this is only an evidence of his worth in the estimation of his fellow-citizens. But we do give honor to the faithful discharge of public trusts, that others may be led to emulate the example. The administration of President Polk has been one of great events, and will form an era in our history. There has been a combination of those events which has scarcely occurred since the organization of the government."

The reception in New York was a grand one. The people were out in vast numbers. One of the newspapers of the day, said: —

" We confess that we admire the man, not less for the stern integrity and purity of his private life, the noble and sterling qualities of his personal character, than for the honorable and commanding station which he holds as the reward of his political integrity, his private virtues, and his personal worth."

Mrs. Polk went as far as Baltimore, where she left the presidential party and travelled west under the care of Mr. Sumner, a young Tennessean, a clerk in one of the departments, whose vacation occurred just at that time. Some members of the party begged her to change her purpose. " Do you want the trouble of having me all through the trip," she asked, " when a separate committee and a separate suite of apartments for my use are always necessary?" " I could not go with Mr. Polk at the receptions," she said to us in relating these experiences, " for he was always with the officials, and I could not stand with him to shake hands with the multitude who crowded to see him, the populace, the working-men, the high and low whom he must receive. In these days opinions and manners are quite different. The ladies go with the gentlemen into all places and all assemblies. In those days it was not thought suitable or dignified for them to be thus prominent and conspicuous."

While visiting her mother, she received the following letter, dated July 4, 1847, Portland, Maine : —

My dear Wife: — After I wrote to you at Lowell on the morning of the 2d inst., I proceeded to this place, where I was handsomely received, and proceeded the same evening to Augusta (the seat of government of the State), and arriving about one o'clock on the 3d, found the capitol and the whole city brilliantly illuminated. On the 3d (yesterday) I had perhaps as gratifying a reception as I have received on my tour. I was received by both branches of the legislature, in the hall of the House of Representatives, and was addressed by the Governor; to which I of course responded, as I think in one of my happiest efforts. Afterwards I was introduced to as many of the immense crowd, and especially of the ladies, as could have access to me. Senator Evans met me at Augusta and behaved very handsomely. At five o'clock I visited his family in the town in which he lives (five miles from Augusta), and afterwards, on a platform erected on the wharf, just before going on board the steamboat to return to this city, Mr. Evans addressed me in the presence of some two thousand persons, male and female, in a very handsome manner and in a very kind spirit, to which of course I responded; and my friends say I made the best speech of the tour. I can give you no more details, but content myself by saying that my whole visit has been of the most gratifying character. The receptions given me by the legislatures and executives of New Hampshire and Maine, in their official character as such, were highly honorable to me, and were all that my friends could have desired. Nothing of a party or of an unpleasant character has occurred anywhere. I reached here about midnight, last night, and have spent a very quiet day, having been twice to church. Mr. Buchanan, Mr. Clifford, Judge Woodbury, Governor Hubbard, General Anderson, Governor Dana, and Governor Fairfield, of Maine, Governor Monten, of Louisiana, Commodore Stuart, besides many members of Congress with whom I have served, have been with me for several days. In a word, I am highly delighted with my visit. On to-morrow, I proceed on my return, dining at Portsmouth (Judge Woodbury's residence); expect to reach Boston at five o'clock, P. M., and proceed immediately to New York, where I will arrive the next morning, and expect to arrive at Washington on Wednesday morning. My health has been good, but my fatigue has been so great that I have been at some times almost worn down, and hence some of the newspapers have represented me to be in bad health.

Mr. Burke tells me he has written to you to-day, and I send you several newspapers, which will furnish you with many incidents connected with my tour, which I have not time or opportunity to write. I have received no letter from you, except the one you wrote at Wheeling. I hope you reached the end of your journey safely, and I calculate that you are to-night with your mother and sister at Murfreesborough.

Your affectionate husband,

James K. Polk.

On the last page, Mr. Buchanan adds a postscript:

" P. S. — I cannot omit this opportunity of presenting you my kindest regards. There was nothing wanting to make our party everything it ought to have been but your presence. We have got along as well as could have been expected in your absence. The President has everywhere been received with enthusiasm, and has played Republican in grand style. He has made a decided impression on New England. One of the prettiest exhibitions on both sides I have ever witnessed came off last evening between him and Mr. Evans, of Maine. The speeches of both were excellent; but I think the President's impromptu reply surpassed the studied effort of the ex-Senator, who has behaved himself extremely well throughout."

A glimpse of familiar scenes, and a re-union with dear friends, was the pleasure of Mrs. Polk's visit to Tennessee; but the trip was mainly taken on account of some items of business. Determining to fix his residence in Nashville at the close of his administration, Mr. Polk had purchased the home of the late Judge Felix Grundy, in whose office he had studied law in his youth. Judge Grundy was, in his day, the most celebrated criminal lawyer in the South, and he had attained high honors also in the Senate of the United States. This purchase was effected by the sale of Mr. Polk's patrimonial estate in Columbia and Maury County, and was not much more than an exchange of residences. The new home was receiving additions and alterations, under the supervision of Mr. V. K. Stevenson, Mr. John B. Johnson, and other of Mr. Polk's friends, and his wife came to suggest whatever changes she might desire. In October a powder magazine west of Capitol Hill was struck by lightning and a terrific explosion appalled the city. The north and west walls of the Polk mansion were so shaken that it was necessary to rebuild them. On her return to Washington Mrs. Polk chose the interior fittings of the house. Knowing the exact dimensions of floors, walls, and windows, she went sometimes to Stewart's establishment in New York City to make purchases,

and sometimes rolls of material were brought to the
White House for her inspection.   In this way, while
gratifying her own taste, she prevented the unwise
outlay of many hundreds of dollars, likely to be
thoughtlessly expended by incautious ordering.

Some time after her return to the capital Mrs.
Polk had the unusual experience of a severe sickness.   A correspondent of the " Baltimore Sun "
writes from Washington: —

" We have a peculiar sorrow in the dangerous illness of
the honored lady of President Polk.   All admire her character, all revere her virtues, and all with one consent join
in supplicating the Father of mercies to spare her long,
very long, to her husband and the friends to whom she is
so dear."

Mrs. Maury, in her volume, " An Englishwoman
in America," says: —

" One morning I found Mrs. Polk reading.   ' I have
many books presented to me by the writers,' said she, ' and
I try to read them all; at present that is impossible, but
this evening the author of this book dines with the President, and I could not be so unkind as to appear wholly
ignorant and unmindful of his gift."

Select parties were frequently invited to dine at
the White House.   On one occasion, there were
twenty-five or thirty literary persons, among whom
was Mrs. L. H. Sigourney.   Mrs. Polk remembered

that she was then rather stout, and had the appearance of one who was thinking, with a straightforward look in her face. Washington is so much farther south than her home in Connecticut, that she spoke of it as a Southern city. Mrs. Alexander Hamilton was also there, and according to the custom of aged ladies of that day, she wore a white cap with a crimped ruffle around the face, and white muslin strings tied under the chin.

An elderly lady, who had been present at this dinner-party, called on Mrs. Polk a day or two afterward, and during the conversation said, " May I take the liberty accorded to ladies of my age, and make a suggestion to you, Madame? " The dining-table at the White House was adorned with a long mirror laid down in the centre of the table, the edges of which were concealed under a border of vines with clustering leaves and blooms, and upon the mirror were placed pyramidal bouquets of flowers, — this arrangement, called the plateau, reflecting the light of the candelabra, and giving an attractive brilliancy to the scene. The table extended about a foot beyond the plateau, and this space was covered with a long napkin, which upon the removal of the dishes for dessert was rolled up by the servants, and formed a bulky bundle of linen. The lady's suggestion was that the long napkin should be cut into short pieces, for the convenience of the servants. "I seldom noticed these things," said Mrs. Polk, "and did not know when the napkin was rolled up and taken off, being engaged in conversation; and I was often so much interested in the stream of discourse that the steward thought I ate too little, and he would put away some dish he knew I liked, hoping I might enjoy it afterward." She said that the servants knew their duties, and she did not undertake the needless task of directing them.

Once when Col. Thomas H. Benton had been invited to dinner, and 6 o'clock, the appointed hour, had passed, he said, " Mrs. Polk, did you not invite us to come and dine at a certain hour? " " Colonel Benton," was the reply, " have you not lived in Washington long enough to know that the cooks fix the hour for dinner? " " Madame," he replied, " you have the advantage of me."

One day, when Daniel Webster was placed beside Mrs. Polk at dinner, Mr. Speight, a senator from North Carolina, was sitting at one end of the table. This was considered an inferior position, the favorite seats being at the middle of the table, where the President sat on one side and his wife opposite, the places on either side of them being filled by guests who commanded the highest respect. Mr. Speight had requested this obscure seat that he might dine quietly, unhindered by company or conversation. Seeing him placed there, Mr. Webster created much amusement by exclaiming, " Is he not a respectable gentleman?"

A pleasant speech made to the mistress of the White House was specially ingenious. In the course of an evening reception, when the rooms were filled with guests, there fell one of those sudden silences that sometimes occur in the midst of the buzz of talk; then a deep, distinct voice slowly said, " Madame, I have long wished to see the lady upon whom the Bible pronounces a woe! " The remark was startling, and no one ventured to make a reply. Mrs. Polk looked with a puzzled air at the speaker, when he continued, "Does not the Bible say, ' Woe unto you when all men shall speak well of you '? "

The company was considerably relieved at this happy turn of so solemn a speech, and the lady bowed her thanks for the delicate compliment.

Mr. Jenkins has preserved in his pages an incident which occurred during a visit made by Henry Clay to Washington, not long before the presidential election in 1848, when he dined at the White House, with many other distinguished men on both sides in politics.

" The party is said to have been a very pleasant

affair; good feeling abounded, and wit and lively repartee gave zest to the occasion. Mr. Clay was, of course, honored with a seat near the President's lady, where it became him to put in requisition those insinuating talents which he possesses in so eminent a degree, and which are irresistible even to his enemies. Mrs. Polk, with her usual frank and affable manner, was extremely courteous to her distinguished guest, whose good opinion she did not fail to win.

" 'Madame,' said Mr. Clay, in that bland manner peculiar to himself, ' I must say that in my travels, wherever I have been, in all companies, and among all parties, I have heard but one opinion of you. All agree in commending in the highest terms your excellent administration of the domestic affairs of the White House. But,' continued he, directing her attention to her husband, ' as for that young gentleman there, I cannot say as much. There is,' said he, ' some little difference of opinion in regard to the policy of his course.'

" 'Indeed,' said Mrs. Polk, ' I am glad to hear that *my* administration is popular. And in return for your compliment, I will say that if the country should elect a Whig next fall, I know of no one whose elevation would please me more than that of Henry Clay.'

"'Thank you, thank you, Madame.'

"'And I will assure you of one thing. If you do have occasion to occupy the White House on the 4th of March next, it shall be surrendered to you in perfect order, from garret to cellar.'

"'I'm certain that —'

"But the laugh that followed this pleasant repartee, which lost nothing from the manner nor the occasion of it, did not permit the guests at the lower end of the table to hear the rest of Mr. Clay's reply. Whether he was 'certain that' he should be the tenant of the President's mansion, or whether he only said that he was 'certain that' whoever did occupy it would find it in good condition, like the result of the coming contest for the presidency, remained a mystery."

Mr. Polk's health, never very strong, began to fail under the heavy weight of his cares and responsibilities. These had been greatly increased by the Mexican war. The Hon. Charles J. Ingersoll called to tell Mrs. Polk that her husband was wearing himself out with constant and excessive application; that if he did not take some recreation, he would die soon after the close of his term; that she must insist upon his driving out morning and evening; that she must order her carriage and make him go with her. "I did so," she

said, " and the carriage waited and waited, until it
was too late. It would have been obliged to wait
all day, for somebody was always in the office, and
Mr. Polk would not, or could not, come. I seldom succeeded in getting him to drive with me,"
she added sadly.

In May, 1848, the Mexican war was brought to a
triumphant close. In the summer the President
visited one or two watering places in Pennsylvania
and Virginia, and the annexed letters were written
at this time by his wife, who was detained by the
presence of guests in the White House : —

" DEAR HUSBAND : — I do hope when you receive this note you will not say to yourself that
your wife is as annoying as the office-seekers, persecuting you wherever you go by compelling you
to open and read a little budget of nonsense of my
own sad complaints that I am separated from
you. Yesterday, not being very well, I kept my
room and felt disconsolate ; everything bore the
appearance of universal quietness. The doorbell
rang only a few times. I beg that you will stay
long enough at Bedford to renovate your health.
Grieved as I may be at your absence (don't think I
am jesting), I do not wish you to leave there before
Monday week ; a shorter time cannot benefit you.
How often do you intend to write me ? "

The annexed fac-simile of a letter of Mrs. Polk was written to her husband in August, 1848. It was enclosed in a small envelope, and then re-enclosed in a larger one. On the end of the latter is the president's endorsement of the date of its receipt.

Saturday
2 O'C.

Dear Husband
               I do hope
when you receive this
note you will not say to
yourself, that your Wife
is as annoying as the office
seekers, persecuting
you where ever you go.
by compelling you to open
and read a little budgett
of nonsense. of my own
sad complaints that
I am separated from you.
        Yesterday not being very
well, I kept my room and
felt disconsolate; Every
thing bore the appearances

of unusual quietness —
The door bell only
rung a few times. —
This morning our friends
got off at last for
Mt. Vernon. —
I beg that you will
stay long enough at
Bedford to renovate
your health. Grieved
as I may be at your
absence, (don't think
I am jesting) I do not
wish you to leave there
before monday week,
a shorter time can
not benefit you.
How often do you intend
to write me?
Your affectionate
Wife Sarah Polk

Two days afterward she wrote as follows : —

"I am this morning distressed on your account
at the change in the weather, fearing that you will
be discouraged and return home without benefit to
yourself. I hope that you will not get sick, and
know that you will keep a *large fire*, and wish that
you may be able to stay as long as you intended
when you left. There is nothing to call your attention back here so soon. I saw Mr. Buchanan last
evening; he was full of the foreign news, but I
learned nothing very specific. I did not go to
church on yesterday. I coughed so much I was
afraid of disturbing the congregation. I would be
very happy to be with you to-day at Bedford. The
visit of our family circle to Mt. Vernon has passed
off very well. The trip to New York and Tennessee is still on the *tapis*, and when they will be accomplished is more than I can tell. I heard from
you verbally on yesterday morning. I fear that
you will be so taken up with the Democracy of
Pennsylvania that you will not find time to write
me. If it rains to-morrow as it does to-day I will
look for you back on Wednesday. *Not* that I think
you ought to come, but knowing you as well as I
do, I fear that you will. I beg you to be patient
and wait for sunshine."

During this summer the portraits of Mr. and Mrs. Polk were painted by Healy. In the year 1847 or 1848 Daguerre's sun pictures were introduced in the United States, and the President and his wife sat for one of the new artists, who came to the White House to solicit their patronage.

In the last winter of this administration gas was brought into the Presidential mansion. It was in use in public buildings, but had not then taken the place of oil-lamps in private houses. The work of putting in the pipes and adjusting the fixtures was troublesome and tedious. Against the remonstrances of several friends, Mrs. Polk insisted that the reception-room should remain as it was, with its elegant chandelier for the use of wax candles. It had become known that at the next entertainment the Executive mansion would be lighted with gas. When the evening arrived, and the house was thronged with guests, lo, the brilliant jets suddenly vanished, and the company was left in darkness. One room, however, was still lustrous with many points of light, — the reception-room, where the wax candles were shedding their soft radiance. There were numerous lively exclamations of pleasure at what was called "Mrs. Polk's sagacity," which in this instance seemed to be a kind of foresight.

MRS. POLK.

Copy of Healy's portrait, painted in 1848.

As his presidential term neared its close Mr. Polk's thoughts turned with longing to the old home in Columbia. The following letter was written in the last month of his administration:

"DEAR MOTHER: — It has been more than four years since I left Tennessee. They have been years of unceasing labor and anxiety, and of high public responsibility. I am heartily rejoiced that my presidential term is so near its close. I am sure that I will enjoy the quiet of retirement, and the rest which I so much need. I expect to leave Washington for Tennessee on the 6th of March, taking the southern route, by the way of Charleston and New Orleans, and will probably reach Nashville about the 25th of March. We will make a short stop at Nashville, and proceed at once to Columbia, when I hope to find you in the enjoyment of good health. My own health and that of my household continue to be good. I write simply to apprise you of my movements at the close of my term."

The same day the appended acrostic was written by " W. S. T.," of Millersburg, Ohio : —

"Joined to no idol save the cause of man,
All critic foes in vain thy deeds shall scan.
Mid storms and clamor and the scowls of war,
Eternal Right hath been thy polar star.

Sacred and just, thy principles sublime,
Known and belov'd, shall spread through every clime.
Preserved by valor from the spoiler's hand,
Our flag still waves o'er freedom's happy land.
Let envy sneer, let calumny decry,
Known to the just, thy fame shall never die."

In the "Ladies' National Magazine" for March,
1849, appeared a tribute to Mrs. Polk, by Mrs.
Ann S. Stephens, who was then in high literary
fame. It was widely copied by the newspapers,
and read by many thousands. We copy only the
third stanza: —

" There, standing in our nation's home,
    My memory ever pictures thee,
As some bright dame of ancient Rome,
    Modest, yet all a queen should be.
I love to keep thee in my mind,
    Thus mated with the pure of old,
When love, with lofty deeds combined,
    Made women great and warriors bold."

A correspondent of the "New York Journal of
Commerce" gave a description of the last reception of the President and his wife, which occurred
on the 28th of February: —

" Although we were old-fashioned enough to go at half-
past eight o'clock, we found a large concourse of the sovereign people already assembled. After exchanging a word
or two with Mr. and Mrs. Polk we passed on into the
well-known East Room. The rooms were lighted up most
beautifully. About one o'clock in the morning the doors
of the Presidential mansion were closed. It is estimated

that more than five thousand people paid their respects to
Mr. and Mrs. Polk in the course of the night. The
greater part of them were strangers who had come to
Washington to witness the inauguration. There were
almost no members of either the Senate or House of Representatives, as both those bodies were in session that night.
Several, if not all, of the members of the Cabinet were
present. I was struck with the very venerable and patri-
archal aspect of Mr. Cave Johnson, the Postmaster-General.
Mr. Buchanan looks very considerably older than he did
four years ago. He informed us that he is going to return
to Lancaster, Pennsylvania, his native place, to spend the
remainder of his life there. They say he has a ' Sabine
farm ' in the vicinity of that ancient but small German city.
Mr. Polk appeared very well. Mrs. Polk appeared, as she
always does, a charming woman, who has won the profound
respect of all hearts. Mr. Polk's administration has been
a most eventful one. During his term the annexation of
Texas was consummated, the vexed question of the northern boundary of Oregon was settled, and the large provinces
of New Mexico and California were added to the United
States as the result of a war that might possibly have been
postponed a few months or years, but which was in my
humble opinion inevitable."

The last State dinner took place on Thursday,
the 1st of March, and was given in honor of the
President-elect, Gen. Zachary Taylor, and the Vice-
President-elect, Mr. Millard Fillmore.

A writer in the "Washington Union" contributed
an eloquent valedictory to the lady whose sojourn
in the capital city was so near its close: —

A FAREWELL TO MRS. POLK.

Lady, farewell! Amid the gloom of grief,
How many a heart will utter that sad sound.
Farewell! For thee a thousand hearts will mourn,—
So much of friendship lost, of sorrow found.
And thou wilt leave a void in friendship's hall,
Where joyous notes were once so wont to rise,
Like that fair pleiad which forsook its home,
And caused to mourn the sisters of the skies.
But thou must go; yet with thee thou shalt bear
A stranger's hope upon the distant way,
And only fade to give a calmer day.
A welcome, too, I 'd give thee to my home,
My sunny home, the old Palmetto soil,
Where many a heart, all warm and true and kind,
Shall chase away the gloom of travel's toil.
And may life pass as soft as sunset hour,
When gentle rays gleam on the skies above,
And may each pulse in sweetest union beat,
To the soft music of the harp of love.

The 3d of March fell on Saturday. After receiving throngs of visitors during the day Mr. and Mrs. Polk withdrew to a hotel at six o'clock, there to remain until after General Taylor's inauguration on the following Monday, when they would begin their journey homeward. They were escorted to the hotel by the members of the Cabinet and their families.

The next day they were at church in their accustomed seats. The pastor, Mr. Ballentine, addressed them in a touching little farewell speech; and when the services were over, instead of dispersing as usual, the congregation stood still, seemingly spell-bound by the universal desire to see the President and his wife. They were the only persons who stepped from their places, and as they moved down the aisle, greeting one friend and another as they passed, the congregation closed in behind them, thus paying a silent homage of sincere respect.

This Sabbath was the 4th of March, and there was much comment made upon the occurrence; some persons supposing that on that day there was no President, Mr. Polk having withdrawn the evening before, and General Taylor being obliged to wait until Monday to be inaugurated. It seemed to be a sort of interregnum. It is the law, however, that every officer's term shall continue until the installation of his successor, and therefore Mr. Polk was the President until General Taylor took the oath of office.

On Monday, according to custom, the out-going President rode to the Capitol in the carriage with his successor, to take a part in the solemnities of the inauguration. Seated beside them were the Hon. Robert C. Winthrop, ex-Speaker of the House, and Mr. Seaton, mayor of Washington. Mrs. Polk witnessed the impressive rites which, four years before, had been so closely connected with her own life.

DEPARTURE FROM WASHINGTON
TO TENNESSEE.

CHAPTER VIII.

1849.

A T nine o'clock on the evening of the 5th of
March, 1849, escorted from the hotel to the
steamer by the members of his own cabinet and
their families, and also by many others, Mr. and
Mrs. Polk took passage on the steamer "Baltimore," for Richmond. They were accompanied by
their young nieces, Miss Hays and Miss Rucker,
by the Hon. Robert J. Walker, ex-Secretary of the
Treasury, Major Daniel Graham and wife, of Nashville, and other personal friends. Mr. Polk had
accepted the invitations of the Southern cities, and
was going homeward by that route. The journey
was marked by receptions, by military displays,
decorations and illuminations, and other manifestations of respect and honor. That these ovations
were prompted by pure esteem is plain from the
fact that Mr. Polk was retiring from power and
had no favors to bestow. Universal approbation
had been freely expressed for the womanly and

sensible course of his wife in the most conspicuous home in the United States, and this feeling
doubtless had a share in the sentiment impelling
these tributes of respect.

The travellers took the railway at Acquia Creek.
At Fredericksburg and other points on the road,
the people were assembled in crowds to greet
them. At the Junction the ex-President was met
by a committee of invitation, who accompanied
him to Richmond. Here the streets and windows
were filled with spectators, and handkerchiefs were
waving in every direction. The booming of cannon,
and the brilliant military display created a scene
of the most exciting character. A committee of
the legislature conducted Mr. Polk to the hall
of the House of Delegates, where the Senate, the
House, with Governor Floyd and Council, and a
large number of citizens had assembled. Mr.
Speaker Hopkins addressed Mr. Polk in a speech
from which the following passage is quoted: —

"I may say that, previous to your administration, the setting sun of heaven never cast his
last evening rays upon the confines of our glorious
Union. But now, sir, and forever, that brilliant
orb of light, when he emerges from the billows
of the Atlantic, darts his first morning rays upon
the sandy beach of our eastern sea-shore, and after

performing his daily round through the heavens, when he dips his broad disk into the placid bosom of the calm Pacific, his last lingering beams still play upon United States soil in the glittering gold-dust of California."

Mr. Polk, in reply, spoke of the great honor done him in so enthusiastic a reception. One of his remarks was that he was no longer a *servant* of the people, but had become now, since Monday last, a *sovereign*.

Mrs. Polk, with the other ladies of the party, had been taken to the residence of Mr. James A. Seddon, and during the few hours of their stay in Richmond they received many visitors, and were well entertained.

At Petersburg, where they dined, and at Weldon, where Whitfield's Hotel and other buildings were illuminated in their honor, they were greeted with great cordiality. When they reached Wilmington, on Wednesday morning, the bells were rung, and a large procession, led by the military with stirring music, conducted them to Swann's Hotel. During the day Mrs. Polk received many callers. Among the crowds who flocked to see Mr. Polk at the Masonic Hall, was the committee sent from Charleston to welcome him in advance to that city. At ten o'clock Thursday morning they left

9

Wilmington on the steamer "Governor Dudley," to the manifest regret of the assembled multitude, and were followed by the parting salutes of the artillery. On the way, the boat stopped for two hours at Smithville. At this place stood an old block-house of the Revolution, identified with the first assertion of Independence; and here many pressed to pay their respects to the out-going President.

Friday morning they landed at Gadsden's Wharf, Charleston. Mrs. Polk and the ladies of her company were conducted by a special committee to apartments prepared for them in the Carolina Hotel. Mr. W. H. Conner offered to the party the hospitalities of the city. He was appropriately chosen for this pleasant duty, having been a fellow-student at Chapel Hill with their honored visitor, and a native of the same county in North Carolina. In the streets there were triumphal arches; private houses were decorated, while the windows and balconies were white with fluttering handkerchiefs. The dense masses of people in the streets raised their hats, as one man, in honor of the city's guest. After a cordial welcome from the mayor and hundreds of citizens, the ex-President and his party were introduced to Governor Seabrook, and to the general, field, and

staff officers of the militia. At four o'clock they
dined at St. Andrew's Hall with the city authorities
and many citizens. Over the entrance to the hall
a temporary stand for the orchestra had been
erected, supported by palmetto pilasters, along the
front of which were painted on white cloth the
arms of North Carolina and of Tennessee. In
the centre, on blue silk, in gold letters, were the
words, "Territories of New Mexico and California." Every window was curtained with the
national flag, except one, where hung the flag of
the State. The window facing the entrance was
surmounted with the great seal of the United
States.

Early the following morning the presidential
party embarked for Savannah. A beautiful canopy had been built on the wharf, under which they
passed to the boat. Two pillars, fifteen feet high,
were made of square bales of Carolina upland cotton, resting upon bases of large Georgia bales, each
pillar faced with a bale of Carolina Sea Island cotton. A barrel of rice capped each pillar. These
were connected by a beam of Carolina pine, covered
with American ensigns in graceful festoons, and supporting this inscription: "The Old Palmetto State
bids thee farewell." The whole was entwined with
branches of arbor-vitæ, laurel, cedar, and palmetto.

It was the law at that time in South Carolina that
if the Governor should go beyond the State lines
he would cease to be the Governor. The original
plan of the party had been to visit the coast towns
of South Carolina, and Governor Seabrook embarked with them; but, unknown to him, it had
been arranged to go directly to Savannah. When
the governor learned this fact he left the steamer at
Beaufort.

About nine o'clock in the evening the vessel was
seen from the bluffs of Savannah, and her signal
rockets and many lights proclaimed the presence
of the distinguished travellers. The guns of the
Chatham Light Artillery, Captain Gallie, saluted
them as the steamer approached, and spoke in
loud tones a Georgia welcome. The " Savannah
Georgian " of March 12, 1849, says: —

" This veteran corps had the pleasing duty of welcoming
with similar tones from their well-plied pieces, the illustrious Washington, when President, to our city and State,
and of receiving the encomiums of the Father of his country, with the gift of two cannon, captured at Yorktown."

When the boat reached the wharf the mayor and
many citizens came on board and were introduced;
after which the distinguished guests were escorted
by a large body of the military to the Pulaski House.
One who saw it all wrote: " As the procession

moved to the hotel, the mellow beams of the full
moon spread over the face of the scene, exhibiting
to the beholder the streets thronged with people,
and the windows and balconies a perfect galaxy of
the pride and beauty of Georgia." Subsequently
the ex-President received the visits of the citizens
at the Armory Hall.

The next day being Sunday, Mr. and Mrs. Polk
went to the Independent Presbyterian Church, of
which the Rev. Mr. Preston was pastor. When
they were seated, hymn-books were passed to them
by various persons, and with every book was a little
bouquet of roses, or violets, or some other fragrant
flower. " We took the bouquets," Mrs. Polk said,
" appreciating the delicately offered compliment,
but returned the books, for we could use but one."

Early on Monday morning, accompanied to the
depot by troops and music, and a host of citizens,
the party took the train for Macon. Reaching that
city at six o'clock in the evening, "they were received," says the "Georgia Telegraph," "with every
demonstration of respect by the crowd who filled
the sidewalks and windows, from which many a
snowy scarf fluttered to the evening breeze." Tuesday morning, the ex-President was welcomed by the
Hon. A. H. Chappell, and Mr. Polk spoke in reply
from an upper porch of the Floyd House. Though

the day was warm many ladies were present, and the attention of all was so absorbed that there was scarcely a movement of the umbrellas. Mrs. Polk was with a group of ladies in the parlor below, within sound of her husband's voice. She said that " the speech was beautifully delivered, as all his speeches were, his manner quiet, calm, and dignified, and his voice soft and melodious, and at the same time clear and commanding." She thought that his talents were undervalued, simply because he was the opponent of so celebrated a statesman as Henry Clay. The next morning at six o'clock, amid the roar of cannon, and the farewell greeting of hundreds who had assembled at that early hour, the party left by the Macon and Western cars.

At Forsyth and Barnesville and Thomaston and many other places, the people seemed anxious to do honor to those who had honored their country by noble conduct in high position. At Columbus they were entertained at the home of Judge Colquitt, the father of Governor Colquitt; and at Montgomery, Alabama, they were greeted with many signs of joyous welcome. From the latter city they took passage in the steamer " Emperor " for Mobile. Here the demonstration was novel and unique. As the steamer approached, the boat carrying the committee of reception came alongside and was lashed fast.

The committee then boarded the steamer, accompanied by a band of musicians, and two Nashville ladies, Mrs. Mason and Mrs. Ledyard, the only persons permitted that privilege, the number already on board being so great. Then the steamers on the bay, gayly decorated, drew near on either side, forming a semi-circle in front of the city. The mayor stood on shore, on a pile of cotton bales as high as a two-story house, and addressed the late President in a glowing speech of welcome, to which Mr. Polk replied from the deck of the steamer. It was a striking scene, and those who saw it can never forget the impression made by the lovely bay reflecting the tints of the bright sky, the fluttering pennons, the decorations of the steamers, and the rich music enveloping the whole like a delicious atmosphere.

Mr. Polk was much weakened by the fatigue and excitement of this triumphal progress. The sudden change of climate in the early spring-time had also reduced his strength. He had long been suffering from impaired health, and a predisposition of late years to severe attacks of illness made it imperative that he should hasten homeward. The dreaded cholera had made its appearance in many places, north and south, and there had already been several cases in New Orleans. Extensive preparations for

a reception had been made in this queen city of
Louisiana. He acknowledged the kindness of the
people by taking part in a public dinner, from
which, however, he withdrew early, in compliance
with the wish and entreaty of his wife. The physician had said to her, " You can insist on leaving
immediately, but your husband cannot do so without seeming to undervalue the honors the city has
been arranging for him."

The trip thus far had been without expense to
the ex-President, but now Mrs. Polk earnestly desired to bear all their own expenses, that they might
be free to leave at once. The committee advised
her, however, that a steamer would convey Mr.
Polk and herself and friends to Nashville without charge; " but, Madame," they said, " it is not
yet ready; but will be on the day appointed
for your departure." While profoundly grateful
for this attention, the feeling that her husband's
life was at stake admitted of no delay; and they
accordingly at once embarked. The original plan
was to stop at Natchez, but Mr. Polk had been
taken ill on the boat, and it was absolutely necessary to hasten homeward. A correspondent wrote:
" Much to the disappointment of the people of
Natchez, the loud report of the brass field-piece
mounted on the bluff overlooking the river, had

scarcely apprised the neighborhood of the near approach of the steamer, ere a gun from the 'Watkins'' deck announced her arrival and departure, and she continued to stem the mighty current of the Mississippi on her way to Nashville."

The illness of Mr. Polk detained the party at Smithland, and they did not reach Nashville until several days after the appointed time.

The " Nashville Union " of April 3 said : —

"The reception of Mr. Polk yesterday, although entirely spontaneous, was one of the most enthusiastic we have ever witnessed. He was expected last Friday, and arrangements for his reception were interrupted by news of his sickness at Smithland. The most intense anxiety for his health has pervaded the city, which was relieved by the intelligence yesterday morning that he would be in Nashville Monday morning. By eleven o'clock the steamboat landing was crowded. The steamer ' Countess ' arrived at our wharf about twelve o'clock, and Mr. Polk was escorted by the multitude to the Court House Square, where he was addressed by Gov. Neill S. Brown, in an eloquent speech. The feebleness of the late President was apparent, and it was scarcely expected that he would do more than make an acknowledgment of the reception. But he seemed to be inspired from the moment the first word fell from his lips, to forget his feebleness, and to renew his ancient energy, as he ' felt his foot upon his native heath.' His speech was touching, and he referred in eloquent terms to the happiness of reaching home. At the conclusion of the ceremonies Mr. Polk was escorted to the

Verandah, where he and his wife were visited by a large number of citizens."

They remained a day or two at this new hostelry, now called the Commercial Hotel.

Their first duty and pleasure was to visit the two loving and proud mothers, Mrs. Elizabeth Whitsitt Childress at Murfreesborough, and Mrs. Jane Knox Polk at Columbia. They were received at Murfreesborough with every mark of esteem, and the people remembered that it was in their town that Mr. Polk had begun a public career in which he had achieved so much for his fellow-countrymen, and distinction for himself. At Columbia he was greeted by the citizens of Maury, Marshall, Giles, and Lewis counties, who met him with music and waving banners. General Pillow made the address of welcome. At the residence of his mother he was met and congratulated by hundreds, of both political parties.

When they returned to Nashville, their new home was ready, and the parlors were thrown open to receive old and new friends. In such pleasant presence and with unbounded expressions of good wishes, the ex-President and his wife took up their abode at Polk Place.

THE NASHVILLE HOME.

EX-PRESIDENT POLK.

CHAPTER IX.

1849–1850.

POLK PLACE was a large and substantial building. A part of the grounds in front of the
south entrance was enclosed in a tall iron fence
with heavy folding gates, while the portion leading
to Church Street was given to the city as a thorough-
fare, and is known as Polk Avenue. The carriage-
drive sweeps round either side of the pavement,
from the gates to the house, in a green lawn formerly dotted with trees. Only a few of these now
remain. Most of them were short-lived, and were
blown down by storms, or worn out by time. Passing up three or four stone steps and across a small
open vestibule, one is ushered through a lofty doorway into a spacious, airy hall, opening into parlors
to the right and left. From this large hall, a smaller
one on the north side leads to the dining-room and
other apartments. Another passage leads to the
east entrance with a wide portico, supported by
fluted columns. The grounds on this side slope

gradually to Vine Street, where the iron gate is formed of a massive anchor, surmounted by the American Eagle. In the centre of the large hall was a circular table covered with a slab of Egyptian marble about three feet in diameter, inlaid with a mosaic of colored marbles, representing the American Eagle bearing the coat of arms of the United States; while in the margin were thirty white stars, the number of States then composing the Union. This slab had been presented by a friend in Tunis, and arrived soon after Mr. Polk reached Nashville. The frame of the table was of dark wood, and was made in Tennessee.

The appointments of the various rooms were tasteful and substantial. But the rich carpets, the damask curtains, and red velvet ottomans, sofas, and easy chairs, and other furniture, were not so attractive as the numerous pictures. Opposite the entrance to the large hall, was an engraving of the Senate Chamber as it was early in the forties, in which the familiar faces of Clay, Calhoun, Webster, and other notable men of that time, are depicted. In the gallery appears Mrs. Madison among the visitors. Mrs. Polk, who was not then in Washington, was also seated in the gallery, without a bonnet, — a piece of absurdity at which she seemed much amused. The most interesting picture in this hall

HERNANDO CORTEZ.

was a portrait of Hernando Cortez, a life-size, three-quarter-length view. Shortly before the close of her husband's presidency it was presented to Mrs. Polk by General Worth, whose monument adorns the angle at the junction of Fifth Avenue and Broadway in New York. It seemed especially appropriate that General Worth, one of the officers in the Mexican army, should send a picture of Cortez, the original conqueror of that country, to the wife of the President under whose administration a large part of this valuable territory was added to the United States. The portrait is a copy of one that hangs in the Hospital of Jesus, founded by Cortez, in the city of Mexico, and represents that hero equipped in shining coat of mail, standing beside a table where lie his iron gauntlets and plume-crowned helmet. His hair and beard are dark and abundant, and the large brown eyes are looking upward with a contemplative expression. On the drapery of the background is the coat of arms which the Emperor Charles V. granted to Cortez by a royal patent issued at Madrid on the 7th of March, 1525. On the 7th of May, 1849, the picture was hung in the hall at Polk Place, and the same day a despatch came announcing the death of General Worth, in San Antonio, Texas.

Over the white marble mantel-piece in the large

parlor was Mr. Polk's portrait, painted by Healy in
1848; and in the recess on the right, that of his
wife, painted at the same time. The latter reveals
to us a graceful woman, with bright, dark eyes, and
clustering curls under a becoming head-dress. She
is attired in red velvet, with uncovered neck according to the custom of that day, while from the right
shoulder a black lace shawl hangs in careless folds.
She is smiling, as if some pleasant word had just
been spoken, or had occurred to her own mind.
In this room were portraits of Washington, Jeffer-
son, and Madison, copies of Stuart's original pictures in Mrs. Madison's house at Washington.
They were copied by Mr. King, of that city, having
been ordered by Mr. Polk after his return to Tennessee, and did not arrive until after his death.
Mrs. Madison died about two months afterward.
There was also a portrait of Governor Aaron V.
Brown, painted by the artist Cooper. Facing
Washington's picture was General Jackson's portrait, painted by Sully. The hair is iron-gray, and
the eyes are lighted with a gentle, kindly expression. Beneath this was an engraving of John
Quincy Adams, whose face is bright with an animated look which he did not often wear in the
presence of Jackson. In a dark, heavy frame was a
fac-simile of the Declaration of Independence, with

all the historic names affixed in autograph. In the smaller parlor across the hall, were portraits of Mr. and Mrs. Polk, painted by Earle during General Jackson's presidency. His first message to Congress, printed on white satin framed in gilt, Mr. Polk had placed on the mantel; and on either side of it was a copy of his inaugural address as Governor of Tennessee, and as President of the United States, similarly printed and framed. These were left just where they had been put by his own hand. An étagère enclosed with glass doors, standing beneath Mrs. Polk's portrait, contained her husband's canes, and also the books which had been presented to her, among which were several fine copies of " The Pilgrim's Progress."

This home was to be a veritable and continuing White House of repose and peace, in which the favored dwellers expected to spend tranquil and happy days, after many years of public life and service.

In the pleasant weeks of the spring-time Mr. Polk's health continued as usual, and he and his wife occupied themselves with their friends and books, and in overseeing the improvements of the grounds around the house. A friend writing at that time says that he lately saw him on the lawn, superintending the removal of some decaying cedars, and adds, "I was struck with his erect bearing and the energy of his manner, which gave promise of long life. His flowing gray locks alone made him appear beyond middle age."

On the 28th of May Mr. Polk wrote to his nephew, J. Knox Walker: "There have been a few cases of cholera here within the past week, some of which have terminated fatally. There is some alarm in the community in consequence of its appearance, though it is not considered as epidemic. We are quietly settled in our new home, and are pleased with it."

A day or two afterward he said to his wife, "Sarah, Nashville is getting so much of the cholera that we will go away Monday." He had bought a pair of carriage-horses, and his last business transaction was to give a check for four hundred and fifty dollars in payment. On Saturday, they drove out to Major Graham's place in the country. Their plan was to leave home on Monday, to pass the night at the house of Mr. George W. Childress, on the way to Columbia. On Sunday morning he was lying on the sofa, downstairs, and said, "Sarah, I cannot go to church with you to-day." She replied, "Well; I will go by myself. You cannot always be with me." When she had left the room, he called her back; "Sarah, I do not

want you to go. I am too unwell. Have a fire
made in my room upstairs, and send for Dr. Felix
Robertson. Tell him I want company to sit with
me this morning." It was the third of June, but
a cool day. On a rainy day, the week before, he
had busied himself in arranging his books, and
absorbed in the labor had overtaxed his strength.
This brought on a return of a malady which had
troubled him for some years.

On Sunday evening Dr. Robertson again called
and suggested that as he was too old to go out at
night, some younger practitioner should be called
in. Dr. Buchanan was employed; and the next
day Dr. Esselman was also engaged. He was an
old friend of Mr. Polk's, and had been General
Jackson's physician, attending him in his last illness, four years before.

For a long time the enfeebled state of his health
had given Mr. Polk much anxiety concerning his
wife. Should he be taken away, his heart sank at
the thought of the desolation of widowhood that
would befall her who had so long been the constant
companion and the sympathetic sharer in the varied
experiences of his life. So perfect had been their
union that he could hardly realize the fact that his
boyhood had been spent without the daily joy of
her presence. He might not be able to spare her

the pain of separation, but he would at least so arrange his affairs that she should still have the refuge and comfort of a home. The straits to which Mrs. Madison had been reduced in her declining days had distressed him, and he was anxious that his wife should be placed beyond the need of public or private beneficence. Soon after the beginning of his illness he said to her that he had so settled the property that it could not be taken from her; that the plantation in Mississippi would support her; but if that income should fail, she could get some friend to take a part of the house and board her. Unwilling to hear him talk on such a subject, she interrupted him, but he persevered in telling her what to do in the event of his death. " How thoughtful he was," she afterward said, " and how far-seeing; for it is owing to his wise precaution that the home which he selected has been to me a sheltering haven through all these years."

His devoted friends, John B. Johnson and V. K. Stevenson, sat at his bedside every alternate night. During these heavy days the cook was taken sick, but Mrs. Polk knew nothing of it, for Colonel Stevenson hearing of the inconvenience, went quickly home and sent his own to Polk Place, hiring a strange servant for his own family. Mrs. Polk learned of this delicate kindness long afterward.

As the disease continued its hold, Mr. Polk asked that his brother-in-law, Dr. Hays of Columbia, be sent for. Dr. Jennings and several other physicians were also summoned for consultation, but all efforts were unavailing; the precious life ebbed slowly but steadily away. One day the public stage stopped at the Avenue, and Bishop Otey alighted. He entered the sick chamber and stood beside the bed. Holding one of Mr. Polk's hands in his, with his own right hand uplifted, he prayed earnestly for the dying man.

A Nashville correspondent of the "New York Herald" gave a detailed description of the closing scenes, from which the following extract is taken:

"Mr. Polk sent for the Rev. Dr. Edgar of the Presbyterian Church, desiring to be baptized by him. He said, 'Sir, if I had suspected twenty years ago that I should come to my death-bed unprepared, it would have made me a wretched man; yet I am about to die and have not made preparation. Tell me, sir, can there be any ground for a man thus situated to hope?' The minister made known to him the assurances and promises of the gospel that mercifully run parallel with man's life. Mr. Polk evinced much knowledge of the Scriptures, which he said he had read a great deal, and deeply reverenced as divine truth. The conversation fatiguing him too much, the baptism was postponed till the next evening. In the interval, he recollected that when he was Governor and lived

here, he used to hold many arguments with the Rev. Mr.
McFerrin, a talented Methodist minister; and that he had
promised him that when he did embrace Christianity, he,
Mr. McFerrin, should baptize him. He therefore sent for
Dr. Edgar, made known this obligation, and expressed his
intention to be baptized by the Methodist minister. The
same day the venerable Mrs. Polk, his mother, a pious
Presbyterian lady, arrived from her residence forty miles
distant, accompanied by her own pastor, hoping that her
son would consent to be baptized by him. ' Mother,' said
Mr. Polk, ' I have never disobeyed you, but you must yield
to your son now, and gratify my wishes.' His wise mother
did not hesitate to give her consent; and in the presence
of Dr. Edgar, and the Rev. Mr. Mack, of Columbia, he
received the rite of baptism at the hands of Mr. McFerrin.

"He continued gradually to sink, and at twenty minutes
before five o'clock, on the afternoon of the 15th of June,
he passed away without a struggle, simply ceasing to
breathe. He was in his fifty-fourth year. About half an
hour before his death his venerable mother entered the
room, and kneeling by his bedside, offered up a beautiful
prayer to the King of Kings and Lord of Lords, commit-
ting the soul of her son into His holy keeping.

"The body lies in state to-day. The drawing-rooms are
shrouded in black; every window is in mourning with
black scarfs of crape; the two pillars before the south
entrance, and the tall columns of the portico facing the
east, are wound with black cloth. Before the funeral,
Masonic ceremonies will be performed in the drawing-
room over the body. Death has impressed the features
with the seal of majesty. A plain silver plate upon the
coffin bears his name, and the dates of his birth and
death."

No words can describe the depth of grief into which the proud and loving wife was plunged by this bitter bereavement. Many years after, recalling the scenes of dignity and joy through which she had passed, she said, pathetically, when she came to this experience, " and life was then a blank."

The funeral sermon was preached in the Mc-Kendree Methodist Church, by Dr. McFerrin. The text was from the first chapter of 1 Peter, verses 3–5 : " Blessed be the God and Father of our Lord Jesus Christ, which according to His abundant mercy hath begotten us again unto a lively hope by the resurrection of Jesus Christ from the dead, to an inheritance incorruptible, and undefiled, and that fadeth not away, reserved in heaven for you, who are kept by the power of God through faith unto salvation ready to be revealed in the last time." From this same text Dr. McFerrin had preached a sermon at a camp-meeting held near Columbia in 1833, at which Mr. Polk was present. Dr. Fitzgerald, in his life of Dr. McFerrin, says: " The plain common-sense and earnest spirit of the sermon commended the truth to the judgment of the clear-headed and honest lawyer, and the Holy Spirit opened his heart to receive the message of God. The gracious impression was indelible. He went away from the camp-ground a convicted sinner, if not a converted man. The words of the sermon still rang in his inner ear, the prayers and songs of the worshipping multitude followed him, and as he rode homeward through the beech forests and fertile fields of Maury County, he was a changed man."

A record of the manifestations of grief, public and private, at the loss of this citizen, patriot, and friend would fill a volume. Mrs. Polk's grief was almost unspeakable. At first, her friends naturally refrained from mentioning the name of her husband. But the Rev. Dr. Philip Lindsley, President of the University of Nashville, when he called to see her, said that it was his custom in conversing with the bereaved to speak of the dead. This directness of speech caused her a pang like the probing of a wound too sore to bear the touch of even a gentle finger. Her tears began to flow, and the relief of speaking freely of that which ever weighed heavily on her thoughts was so soothing that she was much comforted by the visit.

The following extract is from one of the many letters of condolence which came from old friends. It was written by the Hon. W. L. Marcy, Mr. Polk's Secretary of War.

"When the awful event was announced I could
scarcely realize its truth. It was too afflicting
to be readily believed; and too well authenticated
to be reasonably doubted. This vacillation between hope and fear soon ceased. When the sad
news could no longer be questioned, all began to
reflect upon the extent of our loss. The memory
of the past was recalled; those incidents which
made him dear to private friendship, those great
events which made him an object of public
consideration, rushed upon our recollection. If
it be true, as is often said, that sorrows are les-
sened by being divided, you will derive consolation from the fact that a whole nation mourns
with you, that numerous friends in every part of
this extensive country deeply sympathize in your
sorrows. The Almighty hand which chastises can
console; and in your case, I sincerely hope the
ministration of comfort from that source may
equal the severity of the affliction."

As the years passed on friends spoke often of
her husband, and his memory being thus contin-
ually recalled in words, the feeling of unbroken
association with him unconsciously grew. This
feeling was increased whenever she entered the
room he had used as an office, where his books
and writing materials were lying just as he had

left them, and appeared to await his return at any moment. And when the monument in the east grounds of Polk Place was finished, and the remains were placed in the vault beneath, the lonely heart was cheered by the thought that he was again near her, and that from her chamber window she could always see his resting-place. On the 22d of May, 1850, the remains were removed from the city cemetery with impressive ceremonies. Among the ministers present was Bishop Otey, and beside him stood Dr. McFerrin, who offered prayer.

The monument was built by the direction of Mr. Polk, and was designed by William Strickland, the architect of the Capitol of Tennessee. It is a small, square, open temple, with plain columns at each corner, on whose slightly ornamented capitals rests an entablature, impressive by the absence of adornment. On the east front is graven, " James Knox Polk, Tenth President of the United States. Born November 2, 1795; Died June 15, 1849." [1]

---

[1] At that time it was a disputed point whether Mr. Tyler's administration as President was to be counted as one with that of General Harrison, or whether each was to be considered a separate Presidential term. General Harrison lived only one month after his inauguration, and Mr. Tyler was the first Vice President whose lot it was to occupy the chair of the Chief Executive. The author of the inscription believed that only one term was to be credited

A few steps on the west side lead up to the
pavement of the temple, in the centre of which
rises a tomb three or four feet high, bearing
on the east side an inscription in black letters:
"The mortal remains of James Knox Polk are
resting in the Vault beneath. He was born in
Mecklenburg County, North Carolina, and emi-
grated with his father, Samuel Polk, to Tennessee,
in 1806. The beauty of virtue was illustrated in
his life; the excellence of Christianity was exem-
plified in his death." On the north side are the
words: "His life was devoted to the public service.
He was elected successively to the first places in
the State and Federal Governments, — a member
of the General Assembly, a member of Congress
and Chairman of the most important Congressional Committees, Speaker of the House of
Representatives, Governor of Tennessee, President of the United States." On the south face
of the tomb is the following: "By his public
policy he defined, established, and extended the
boundaries of his country. He planted the laws
of the American Union on the shores of the Pacific.
His influence and his counsels tended to organize
the national treasury on the principles of the

to Harrison and Tyler, and so made Mr. Polk the tenth President.
That opinion has since been reversed.

Constitution, and to apply the rule of freedom to navigation, trade, and industry."

This epitaph was prepared by the Hon. A. O. P. Nicholson. A part of it was taken from the official announcement of Mr. Polk's death made to the Court of England by George Bancroft, the resident American Minister.

The fourth side of the tomb was left blank for the epitaph of Mrs. Polk, for whose remains a place had been reserved in the vault below.

Mr. Polk's last will and testament gave to his wife everything he possessed except Polk Place, which was devised to her for life. Near the close of the instrument, he makes this tender mention of her: "I have entire confidence that my beloved wife, Sarah Polk, who has been constantly identified with me in all her sympathies and affections, through all the vicissitudes of my public and private life, for more than twenty-five years, and who by her prudence, care, and economy, has aided and assisted me in acquiring and preserving the property which I own, will at her death make a proper and just disposition of what property she may then possess."

Mrs. Polk was named in the will as executrix, without bond; and Judge John Catron and Major Daniel Graham, executors, clearly with the view

of her thus obtaining the benefit of their advice.
These two friends, with Col. V. K. Stevenson and
Mr. John B. Johnson, true to the wife as they
had been to the husband, attended to her business
affairs.

THE CHANGED LIFE.

CHAPTER X.

1849–1860.

M RS. POLK'S mother, a remarkably sensible and kind-hearted woman, deeply realized the loneliness of her daughter in her widowhood. The eldest son of Mrs. Childress, and also his wife, had died many years before, leaving one little girl, whom the affectionate grandmother had taken and reared as her own child. In the course of time this little girl became Mrs. Jetton; and when she died, several years afterward, Mrs. Childress took the youngest child, a daughter, to care for as she had cared for the mother. This little great-granddaughter, Sarah Polk Jetton, Mrs. Childress brought to Nashville, and committed her to the care of Mrs. Polk, in the hope that the sunny presence of childhood might enliven the then desolate home. Mrs. Polk gratefully accepted the kindness of her mother, and the more gladly as she could thus fulfil the dying request of her niece, that she would interest herself particularly in the welfare of the child. " Judge Catron was well acquainted with my tastes," said

11

Mrs. Polk, " and once said to me, ' You are not the one, Madame, to have the charge of a little child; you, who have always been absorbed in political and social affairs.' But," she continued, " Sallie had a good nurse who took excellent care of her, and I have never regretted her coming." It is difficult to imagine how one might have been affected by circumstances that did not occur. However it might have fared with her, living uncheered by the devotion of any near and beloved one, certain it is that the little niece brought a new light and life into the echoing halls and stately parlors of the now quiet mansion.

As the years went by, Mrs. Polk was interested and diverted with her niece's studies and experiences at school; with the visits of her youthful companions, and the gayeties of her young womanhood. Miss Sallie Polk, as she was familiarly known, subsequently married a young merchant of Nashville, Mr. George William Fall, whose family came of good old English stock. He did not take his bride from the home she had so long known and loved, and Polk Place received a new element of brightness in the presence of a business man with his breezy touch of out-door life. Soon a little daughter, Saidee Polk, filled the house with the gladness and cheer of childhood and youth.

The Rev. Dr. Edgar, pastor of the First Presbyterian Church, was desirous that Mrs. Polk
should remove her membership from Columbia to
the church at Nashville. He was a man of high
character and excellent judgment, and felt that such
a change would add to her comfort. Whenever he
spoke to her concerning such a change, she would
pleasantly reply, " Dr. Edgar, I do not wish my
name to be read out in church, in a certificate of
good standing." It was customary to call letters of
dismission, transferring membership from one church
to another, "certificates of good standing." Soon
afterward the Presbyterian Church in Columbia was
burned, and then Dr. Edgar playfully remarked,
" Now, Madame, you will be obliged to join us,
because the list of members in your church was
burned, and in restoring the list from memory your
name was left out, and now you do not belong anywhere." Shortly after, she removed her membership to Nashville, where she remained ever afterward
a faithful communicant.

It was customary for the members of the State
General Assembly to call in a body upon the widow
of the ex-President on New Year's Day. The time
of this visit was subsequently changed by a joint
resolution of the two Houses, to " any suitable day
during the session." The military companies and

other organizations of the city, and all bodies con-
vening here, religious, educational, political; the
Grand Lodges of Masons, Odd Fellows, and
Knights of Pythias, — all made it an order of business,
or rather of privilege, to visit the tomb of the ex-
President, and to pay their respects to his widow.
The firemen in their annual parades marched by
Polk Place, as did all other civic and military processions, with uncovered heads. Sometimes the
military companies paused to salute, which was
always pleasantly acknowledged by the recipient,
who with her friends came down to the gate to
watch the procession.

In the summer of 1859 a member of the Chatham
Artillery, then commanded by Captain Claghorn,
wrote to the "Savannah Republican" an account of
their reception in Nashville. After speaking of the
cordial greeting given them by the crowds of citizens, the local military organizations, and the cadets
from the Military Institute, and of the address of
welcome by the mayor of the city, and of the visit
to the Capitol, where from the western front a salute
of thirty-three guns was fired, — he says: "Returning from the hill to our hotel, we passed the residence
of Mrs. James K. Polk. In the flower-garden in
front of the house, rises a monument erected over
the remains and to the memory of her patriotic

husband, who died ten years ago to-day. As we
marched by, a feeling of sadness seemed to over-
come the whole corps, and as we came to present
arms, we knew that we were paying but a small token
of the respect we felt to the memory of one who
once occupied so elevated a position."

Bishop Green, of Mississippi, was a college-mate
of Mr. Polk's, as was also Bishop Otey, of Tennessee.
Once when in attendance upon a convention of the
Episcopal Church in Nashville, they came with
several of their friends to visit Mrs. Polk. During the conversation she said to Bishop Green,
"Were not you and Mr. Polk rivals?" With a
low bow he replied, "Madame, your husband had
no rival." "That was a handsome answer," she
remarked in recounting this incident. "Some persons would have said, ' Yes, he excelled in this, and
I excelled in that,' trying to make out a good case
for themselves, and showing in what studies each
deserved credit. Not so Bishop Green. Mr. Polk
won the highest honors and the bishop was second."

Having long been identified with the life and
progress of the country, Mrs. Polk was fully prepared to appreciate the labor of all those who gave
themselves to historical studies. The patient col-
lectors of facts and incidents, of relics and other
articles that illustrate the past to future generations,

always won her appreciation.   To the Tennessee Historical Society she gave several objects worthy of preservation.   Among them a medallion likeness of President Polk; a blue pitcher used in the Indian Council convened at Hopewell in 1785, which was called the pitcher of the chief, and originally belonged to Oken–Shan–Tah, the great king of the Cherokees; and also an Indian pipe and ornaments, which had been presented to President Polk by Wee–no–shick, head chief of the Winnebagoes. To these were added the following articles: "The Four Gospels in Choctaw," by Rev. Cyrus Bryington, 1845; a piece of live oak from the old ship Constitution, carved in the form of a book; a hickory cane, presented to President Polk by the " Castile Hickory Club," New York ; and a medallion likeness of Louis Philippe, 1846.

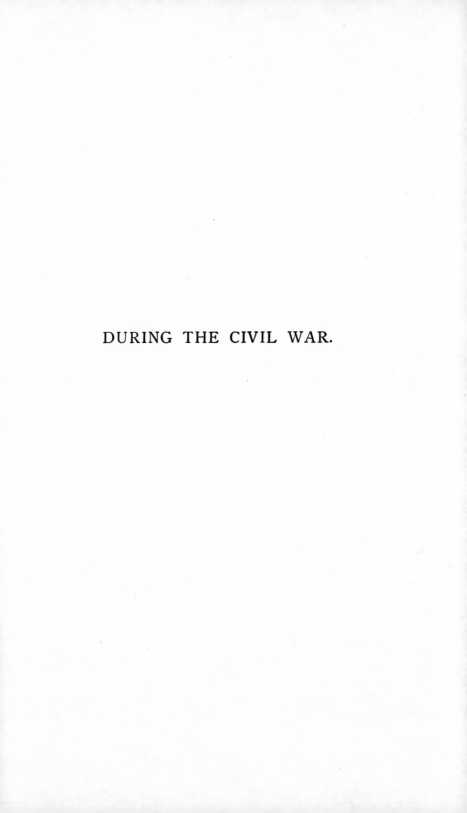

DURING THE CIVIL WAR.

CHAPTER XI.

1860–1865.

SAD and disastrous, the air full of farewells to the dying and mournings for the dead, the Civil War, in its disappointments and terrors, proved to Mrs. Polk the wisdom of Providence that had removed her husband from participation in its direful scenes. He was relieved from the necessity of deciding between the two parts of his country, — as painful a necessity as that of deciding between two children, with one of whom he must go, and to the other he must become an alien. This inexorable necessity filled with agony many a public servant whose life service had been given to the Republic of Liberty, and whose success and happiness had been identified with that of the whole United States. Mr. Polk was naturally a Union man, having devoted himself to the advancement of the whole country over whose government he had presided. But it would have caused him unspeakable distress to take sides against his beloved home. Or if he had cast his lot with his own State, painful in the extreme it would have been to him to see riven asunder the country in whose service he had worn himself out. In either case, he would have been misunderstood, and possibly maligned, and would surely have drunk a bitter cup of sorrow. *She* saw that it was better as it was.

When the Federal army was approaching to take possession of Nashville, some of her near relatives living in Murfreesborough, fearing for her welfare, were urgent that she should go south. They felt that it was not proper for an unprotected woman to remain in a city invaded by a victorious army, and to incur the risks which, to the alarmed and excited imaginations of the people, seemed indeed frightful. They also thought that she was in danger of having her house seized by the military commanders, and of being compelled to leave her chosen retreat. She told them that she was at home, and intended to stay at home, and that if her house should be blown up or burned up, she would pitch a tent on the lawn beside Mr. Polk's tomb, and stay there. In this determination, she was guided by the wisdom of Providence. The officers stationed in the city treated her with the utmost deference. The Confederate commanders who were in Nashville before its occupation by their opponents, and the Federal

generals afterward were alike in their respectful
kindness and manner toward her. This was not
solely attributable to the universal esteem in which
she was held, but arose in a great measure from the
strong common-sense and fine tact she always displayed. In asking for passes or other favors, she
never demanded them as a right, but said, " If I
have asked for anything which it would be incon-
sistent or improper to grant, of course I will not
expect to receive it." Her requests were courteously accorded. When her mother was taken ill,
an officer, with a guard and ambulance, was detailed
to take her to Murfreesborough. The only instance
of her travelling on Sunday was when a special train
was to come on that day from Murfreesborough to
Nashville, and she accepted the invitation to return
with it because of the uncertainty and irregularity
attending the running of trains. Several officers
stationed at Murfreesborough subsequently took
upon themselves the kind duty of acquainting her
from time to time with the state of her mother's
health.

Judge John M. Lea was one of the committee
appointed, with the mayor, to meet the Federal
army on its entrance into the city. He asked Mrs.
Polk, " What shall I say to General Buell for you ? "
" Tell him I am at home," was the reply. This was

said cheerily, in the effort to look at the matter in the brightest light, and seemed to be the best, and indeed the only thing she could say, inasmuch as nothing that anybody said could in any way alter the state of affairs. A few days after his arrival, General Buell, as the commander-in-chief of the Federal army, sent a note requesting permission to call with some friends and pay his respects to the widow of an ex-President of the United States. She replied in writing that she would see him and his friends the next morning at eleven o'clock. At the hour appointed, the general came with several of his staff-officers, and nearly every commanding general in and around the city, eighteen or twenty in number. She had invited a few neighbors to assist in entertaining her visitors, and the interview of an hour was courteous and pleasant on both sides. Upon retiring, the officers expressed their gratification at their kind reception. Elias, the negro man who had waited on President Polk at the White House, was standing at the steps, below the portico, when they took their leave, bowing with uncovered head as had been his custom in the old days in Washington. One of the generals, as he passed out, said, "Well, my colored friend, what do you think of the situation?" "I'm for the rights of the South in the territories," promptly replied Elias.

This unexpected answer raised the hearty laughter of the whole party as they went down the gravel walk, and one of them said, " You 'd better not ask another darkey his political opinions in this section of the country."

All the commanding officers at different times stationed in Nashville also called to honor the memory of a former Chief Executive, and show their respectful regard for his widow. Among these were Generals Thomas, Grant, and others. On one occasion, when Mrs. Polk entered the parlor to receive General Sherman, he remarked that he had been looking at President Polk's Inaugural Address, which not only contained expressions of attachment and loyalty to the Union, but also affirmed that it should be preserved forever indissoluble. " Those are good sentiments, sir," was her reply. General Sherman asked her, " If you were now to visit Washington, Madame, where would you go first? " The reply, which came instantly, seemed to surprise him. " I would go to the White House, sir, to call on the President." Aware of the intensity of public feeling, he possibly thought that the Southern woman before him would express an aversion for Mr. Lincoln and everything pertaining to the Federal Union. She was indeed truly devoted to her own land and

people, but the principles of truth and honor
which she held preserved her from bigotry and
partisanship.

One day an officer came to see her whose grandfather she had known as a member of Congress.
In speaking of her patriotism she said to him that
she felt an attachment for the United States which
was but natural in one who had been identified with
one of its Chief Magistrates, and who had regarded
the whole, and not a section of it, as her native
land. " But how do you think I felt when the battle raged near Murfreesborough, my native home?"

" Madame, if you had not then felt as a Southern
woman would feel whose home was invaded, I could
not have come to see you."

An interesting visitor came one morning, in the
person of General Lytle, the author of that touching poem, "I am dying, Egypt, dying." The
servants chanced to be out of the way, and the
lady went herself to the door. When he saw her
approaching, he exclaimed, " Mrs. Polk!" and
stepping back a few paces, he took off the cloak
hanging around his shoulders, and putting it over
his arm, bowed in the most courtly manner while
introducing himself. When they were seated he
told her that though she did not know him, he had
had the pleasure of seeing her. His father had

been a member of Congress, and had boarded in
the house with Mr. and Mrs. Polk in Washington;
and on one of their journeys, as they passed
through Cincinnati, his father's carriage was sent
for them, and he, a little boy, took delight in sitting beside the driver and getting down to open the
door for the distinguished guests, who had no idea
who he was.

A short distance south of Nashville was Belmont,
the beautiful country home of Mrs. J. A. S. Acklen,
afterward Mrs. Dr. W. A. Cheatham. Her husband was then absent, attending to their plantations
in Louisiana. Her house was partly occupied by
army officers, who advised her, in preparation for
a battle soon to take place in the neighborhood, to
put her valuables in some place of safe keeping. A
large number of portraits and other fine paintings,
with boxes of silver, jewelry, and diamonds, were
sent to Mrs. Polk with the request that she would
take charge of them. The Tennessee Historical
Society also made Mrs. Polk the custodian of some
of its possessions. The soldier who had brought
Mrs. Acklen's valuables, asked if Mrs. Polk would
like to have a guard; to which she replied, "Oh,
no." Her character was her citadel, and she needed
no defence of armed men. In those trying times,
she seemed equal to every occasion; and this signal

power she ascribed to that Divine protection which had kept her safely day by day. She often said that she could not be grateful enough for the guidance which had led her through life, giving her every comfort and advantage. And, certainly, not the least of her blessings was this thankful appreciation of the Divine goodness.

The results of the war left her in altered circumstances, for her financial losses were heavy. Her slaves were freed, her cotton destroyed by fire, and her plantation in Mississippi much depreciated in value. So great was the difficulty of making the cultivation profitable, that she disposed of it, — at first selling a part, and subsequently the remainder of the estate. The affairs of the plantation were honorably and satisfactorily wound up by Judge Avent, the husband of Mary Childress, her niece.

When the war was over, and the legislature again met, the customary call at Polk Place was revived. Col. Bailie Peyton, of the committee appointed to inform Mrs. Polk of the proposed visit, wrote her a note, from which the following sentences are taken : —

" The General Assembly is mainly composed of those who well remember your association with the distinguished personages of a past generation. How nobly you bore your part is attested by the unanimous voice of all. We would not recall the events of the last few years, but it is impossible that we could be insensible to those incidents, which history will preserve, when, as we trust, the calamities of that period are remembered no more. You were in the line of the advancing and receding hosts, in the very gulf-stream of the war, but the mad passions engendered by the conflict were ever calmed in the presence of your abode. Without reference to the flag he followed, each subaltern and superior regarded your feelings as sacred, and his good sword as pledged no less to your defence than to the cause in which he drew it. Candor, Madame, compels us to say that we cannot dissever our veneration and regard for yourself from the grateful recollections we cherish for the memory of your distinguished husband. That spot which holds his remains, that tomb which is watched by such devoted affection, must be sacred in our eyes; it will be doubly so to posterity at a time, far off, as we trust, in the distant future, when your ashes shall mingle with his."

12

YEARS OF GRACIOUS HOSPI-
TALITY.

CHAPTER XII.

1865–1884.

A S in ante-bellum days, so after the war, various organized bodies, local and visiting, made it a point to call on the lady at Polk Place. She was assisted in these receptions by her niece, Mrs. Fall, and other ladies, and a few gentlemen. An address was usually made by some one of the visitors on behalf of the body represented, and a reply on behalf of the honored lady, by some one of the home guests.

On one occasion, during a visit of the General Assembly, Senator Gibson said, " Mrs. Polk, allow me to propose an impromptu toast to our country, to George Washington who did more than any other man to establish it, and to James K. Polk who did more than any other man to enlarge it." The venerable representative from Madison, Robert I. Chester, then moved that " this House do now adjourn until ten o'clock to-morrow," which was received with laughter, and all retired highly pleased.

Some years afterward Mrs. Polk gave to Colonel Chester the heavy walking cane presented to her husband in 1846 by Mr. Joseph Hall, a member of Congress from Maine, which had been cut from the live-oak timber of that stout and famous old vessel, "Ironsides."

In December, 1884, Colonel Chester was the bearer of the electoral vote of Tennessee to the National Senate, and as his ninety-first birthday occurred the July previous, his long journey and important mission made him an object of much attention. Finishing his patriotic business in Washington, he went to Albany to visit President-elect Cleveland. As he passed through Nashville on his return home, he told Mrs. Polk that he had carried the cane she gave him, and that it had everywhere introduced him to the best people.

At a council of the Teachers' National Association, held in Nashville, General Eaton offered a resolution, "that this body call at the residence of Mrs. President Polk in recognition of the eminent position to which her late husband and companion in life was called, as well as out of respect to her womanly qualities." Ex-Governor Foote of Mississippi said: "Nothing could be more proper and becoming, in my judgment, than that this learned and truly National Association should call upon this noble lady. In approaching the abode where she has so long resided in quiet dignity, you will pass in sight of her husband's tomb. Twenty years ago I was appointed to deliver the funeral oration in honor of Mr. Polk in the capital of the nation, a task painful yet pleasing. So now, it will afford me gratification to have the honor of introducing you, sir, and your associates to Mrs. Polk; but while doing so I shall feel, as I never fail to do when I behold her, a natural regret that so much excellence, displayed alike in peace and amid the troubled scenes of war, in high public position, and amid the endearments of domestic privacy, must in a few years more be compelled to bid adieu to earth and its transitory scenes of fancied glory."

Mrs. Polk received many pressing invitations to visit the Centennial Exposition of our national independence at Philadelphia. Colonel Scott, President of the Pennsylvania Railroad, offered to place a palace car at her disposal during her stay. At the same time Colonel Forney, of that city, sent her an urgent request to become his guest. The invitation was sent by Colonel Forney through General Pennypacker of the regular army, then on duty in Nashville. Her friends were desirous that she should accept the courteous generosity of Colonel Scott and others, and make a journey which seemed to promise so much enjoyment, but she could not be persuaded to leave her home. She had been earnestly requested by different Presidents, to spend some time in the Executive Mansion. President Johnson, especially, had sent her a cordial invitation to visit the White House, and meet the friends of former times, and see the changes that had been wrought in her old home. All these proposals she declined. With the exception of brief visits, made at long intervals, to her mother at Murfreesborough, she remained continuously in the beloved home chosen and prepared for her by her husband. Her mother died during the war, at the age of eighty-two, and after that event nothing could tempt her from Polk Place. Here she found ample occupation, and felt no need of seeking satisfaction elsewhere. The family circle was complete with her niece and nephew and their daughter. There were many friends who kept her in full sympathy with the life in the city beyond her own doors. She did not return visits; and went only to church, where her place was always filled when the weather and her health permitted. Many old acquaintances passing through Nashville came to renew former associations; and strangers of all classes constantly called to pay their respects to her. They found her alive to the stirring questions of the day, not clinging, as they might have supposed, to the dead issues of the far-off past when she lived in the midst of the activities of the nation. She was abreast with the news of the hour, familiar with the names of public men and the discussion of public measures, and interested in the drift of public sentiment and the ever-changing condition of affairs. Remembering the great men and the important events of a former generation, she was keenly observant of the men and the movements of the present time.

In August, 1877, the American Association for the Advancement of Science met in the Capitol at Nashville in their twenty-sixth annual session. On the second day Professor Simon Newcomb, the President, made the following announcement: " The city of Nashville rejoices in something which heretofore we have been accustomed to associate only with the ancient world. At this shrine all visitors are expected to worship. In accordance with this custom, which I am sure every one present will recognize as becoming and appropriate, the Association will to-day, at the close of sectional business, proceed to pay their respects to Mrs. Polk, relict of the late President Polk."

Being ushered, at one o'clock, into the large parlor where, with a few friends, Mrs. Polk was

waiting to receive them, President Newcomb said:
" Mrs. Polk, we appear before you as students of
Nature in all her kingdoms, the humble disciples
of a school of teachers whose instructions have rev-
olutionized society, and whose discoveries have
enriched the world. We come as pilgrims of ancient Greece came to the Temple of Diana, to do
homage at your shrine. If the customs of the
world had not changed, our fatted lamb would be
sacrificed on your altar, and the smoke of our in-
cense would perfume the air of your dwelling. By
an expression of our sentiments more modern in its
character, we assure you of our respectful regard
for the consort of one who has filled the highest
position in our land, and who, by the elevation of
her character, commands the esteem of every citizen of her country. We pray, honored Madame,
that Providence may preserve your life and health
through years to come; and that you may long
rejoice in the place you hold in the hearts of your
countrymen."

A fitting response was made by Dr. John Berrien
Lindsley, secretary of the local committee.

The following month the National Association of
Fire Engineers, representing twenty-one States, met
here; and the next afternoon they went in procession from the Capitol to Polk Place, headed by

their president, Capt. William Stockell. Mrs. Polk
said, in her quiet manner, that the visit of the Fire
Chiefs gave her much pleasure. " You, gentlemen,
are the protectors of the lives and property of the
people of this country. I thank you, one and all."
Several spirited songs added to the enjoyment of
all present. In the evening a banquet was given
at the Maxwell House, by the Board of Under-
writers, and among other decorations of the din-
ing-hall was the flag presented to the old volunteer
company, No. 4, by President Polk, of which company he was an honorary member.

President Hayes and Mrs. Hayes visited Mrs.
Polk during their southern tour in the autumn of
1877. They were accompanied by Secretary
Evarts and his two daughters, and also by Col.
Wade Hampton, and Postmaster-General Key.
Mrs. Polk thought Mrs. Hayes a charming woman.
A reception was given to the presidential party by
Col. E. W. Cole and his wife at their residence, but
in accordance with her long-settled habit of refus-
ing all invitations, the lady of Polk Place was not
present.

During a call made by General Sam F. Cary,
when he came to Nashville to deliver two public
addresses, she said to him, " Judge Hoadley of
your city, and the great lawyer, Charles O'Conor,
called on me recently. Mr. O'Conor is, like my-

self, getting along in years, and his hair is snow-
white. We had a good talk of Washington life
away back in the forties when Mr. Polk was President. He told me of his exalted opinion of himself
and his exquisite sensations of distinction and pleasure when he was invited to a public dinner at the
White House. He asked me if I remembered the
occasion. I regretted that in such a multitude of
dinners and social amenities I could not recall the
instance. Mr. O'Conor reminded me of it by saying: 'Why, Mrs. Polk, you and I were young and
jovial then, and I remember it as distinctly as if it
were but yesterday; and you were so gracious to us
all.' His memory was tenacious and enthusiastic,
and I was pleased; but recollection of that particular event was effaced by time."

In the spring of 1880 occurred the centennial of
he city of Nashville. The celebration began on
the hundredth anniversary of the day on which
the settlers of Nashborough on the Cumberland
River entered into " a compact for their self-gov-
ernment and protection." The military, with music
and banners, quaintly uniformed soldiers of a century past, and companies in the more familiar mar-
tial array of the present, display-wagons, trades-
unions, societies, and orders, with citizens on foot
and in carriages, made a long and imposing procession winding through the city. Multitudes thronged

the Capitol grounds, where the bronze statue of
Jackson was to be unveiled. After the manner of
Nashville processions, the ex-President's home and
tomb lay in the line of march. Mrs. Polk was at
the Vine Street gate, and around her were gathered
the youths and maidens of the Grammar Department of the public schools. As the procession was
approaching, the fresh, sweet voices of the girls and
boys, led by their singing-master, struck up the
stirring air of a Centennial Hymn. The following
are two of the stanzas: —

> " The light of vanished days returns
>   To shine once more in Nashville's sky,
> And with the added glory burns
>   Of all the hundred years gone by.
> And lo, this motto — like the sign
> That beamed from heaven on Constantine —
>   These mystic rays from other days
> Emblazon on each grateful heart,
> With more than mortal power or art,
>   ' Give God the praise ! '

> " The air is full of whisperings weird,
>   The echoes of a hundred years.
> The wild war-whoop that brave men feared
>   Comes, dulled by distance, to our ears ;
> Then sounds of busy life and trade,
> When here sweet Peace her dwelling made ;
>   Then waves of song re-echo long
> A people's grateful thanks to Him
> Who led them from the forest dim,
>   And made them strong."

On one of Senator Bayard's visits to Nashville his daughters were with him, and when they called to see Mrs. Polk, Senator Gorman of Maryland, who came with them, remarked to her: "You do not remember me, Madame, but I remember you perfectly. I have opened the door for you many a time when I was a page at the Capitol in Washington."

The Rev. Dr. Peschau, a former pastor of the German Lutheran Church in Nashville, and an enthusiastic member of the Tennessee Historical Society, after removing to Wilmington, North Carolina, wrote a letter from which the following passage is taken: —

"DEAR AND HIGHLY ESTEEMED MRS. POLK: Greetings in the name of our dear Lord Jesus Christ! ... Last week I spent a few days in Charleston, to attend the annual convention of the Lutheran Synod of South Carolina. It was my good fortune to be assigned to the house of William Kirkwood, Esq., a venerable man, eighty-four years of age. How well he remembers Mr. Polk's visit to the city on his return from Washington. It so happened that Mr. Polk was compelled to wait almost an hour directly in front of Mr. Kirkwood's house and under his shade trees, until the military which had come to escort him and a part of his cabinet to the Charleston Hotel had formed in line. The ladies, seeing this, gathered upon the piazza in the second story and fairly showered flowers upon him and his carriage. Mr. Polk thereupon turned and acknowledged the compliment by removing his hat and bowing to them, a recognition they did not expect, and which pleased them all the more. The ladies present on that occasion have often spoken of this incident, and Mr. Kirkwood was delighted to tell me of it, as one who knew you and had visited the resting-place of Mr. Polk. The few ladies of that crowd now living would take pleasure in strewing flowers on Mr. Polk's grave, if they were near it."

Soon afterward Dr. Peschau delivered an address before the Historical and Scientific Society of North Carolina, having for his subject the lady whom he so much admired. A short extract from this address is appended : —

" Mrs. Polk enters, a tall, stately, graceful lady. With beaming countenance and dignified manner, she gives us a welcome that is so different from the stiff, studied superiority of some would-be-great-ones, that we are at a disadvantage and she must come to our rescue, and she does. Such a clear mind, such choice, chaste language; the rapid flow of thought, the vivacity of expression; her animation throughout; the quick wit; the rapid comprehending of what is said, and the ready answer, — all interest us, charm us. Her knowledge of the times, her recollections of the past, how accurate! You are in the presence of a remarkable woman. You leave with reluctance. You feel you have found a true woman. Your heart will praise if your lips do not. You remember your visits, and so does she. She oft-times asked us as to the welfare of those who had previously called, and sometimes even recalled their names and some of their remarks. She is not like the flippant conversationalists often found, but sensible, thoughtful, intelligent. She does not rest in being admired, or seek to court and call forth your studied compliments, but loses herself in her admiration of all that Mr. Polk did that was noble. It was, in our opinion, a wise Providence that permitted him to die, and her to live. We believe this view will become the verdict of unprejudiced history. When Presidents settle down in private life the public forgets them. So it would have been with Mr. Polk. In a hundred ways his reputation could be better kept by his wife than by himself. In honoring him, it was her heart's unselfish, holy devotion, and love's work, and no one would censure her for

that. The various elements of her well-rounded
character have led or helped to lead to the laying
of a thousand wreaths of praise on the grave of
Polk. She outlived whatever animosities, mistakes,
or failures he may have caused or made politically,
and her own good name has given lustre to the
name of her noble, dead husband, whose life in so
many respects was a model, and who lived and died
a good man. Aback of all the public manifestations
of her excellent character, we find that all their
motive powers centre in a Christian heart. In our
last interview, she spoke of her anticipated departure, as only a Christian can speak of death, and
amid the quotation of Scripture verses, and the
expression of Christian sentiments, she uttered the
following, which we have used as the basis of a few
lines in poetical form: ' Yes, Dr. Peschau, I 'm
growing old, I grow old willingly; I grow old not
unwillingly.'

" And now, Mr. President, I will close with the
lines, —

> " The deepening shades, the fading light,
> The chilling air, proclaim death's night;
> But through the gloom light streams to me,
> And I grow old quite willingly.

> *Chorus :* I 'm growing old quite willingly,
> Heaven beckons me to rest so free,
> Hence I grow old quite willingly.

13

" Fair memory weaves its wreaths of gold
    Around the days, the times of old,
    And brings glad childhood back to me,
    Still I grow old quite willingly.

" A nation paved the years with flowers,
    And golden made, with praise, the hours ;
    But honors great no more charm me,
    I 'd rather grow old willingly.

" My strength now wanes, my step grows slow,
    But love for rest and Heaven doth grow ;
    I scarce can wait ; do not blame me
    For growing old so willingly.

" Soon 't will be o'er, life's race be run,
    My duties all and work be done ;
    Near him I love I long to be,
    And grow old now quite willingly.

" Willing to live, willing to die,
    I wait my time from earth to fly, —
    With God and friends in Heaven to be ;
    This helps me grow old willingly."

To these verses Dr. Peschau composed a simple
air, which is cheerful with an undertone of sadness.
The song is dedicated "to Mrs. James K. Polk, a
nation's favorite." She remembered the conversation which suggested the song. When she remarked
that she was growing old cheerfully, that she was
willing to be old, he looked at her intently, as if
impressed by her words, and said, " Mrs. Polk, that
is the poetry of life."

She often earnestly expressed the conviction that God was taking care of her, and leading her gently down the slopes of old age. She was full of thankfulness to the gracious Providence that had given her so many comforts and joys, and in the midst of attentions and adulations sufficient to turn her head, she never forgot that all her favors came from above. Fond of social pleasures, she had always been mindful of the Divine hand by which she was upheld, and was ready at any moment, to sing from the depths of her heart, the old line, " Praise God from whom all blessings flow." This spirit made her so cheerful that no one ever grew sad in her presence. " Why should I feel sad," she said, " when I have been blessed with so happy a life? I am ready to go, and I am willing to stay."

She outlived nearly all her contemporaries. Being asked, on one occasion, if there were many men then living who were in public life when she was in Washington, she replied, " No, very few. There is Gen. Simon Cameron, though. How well I remember him! He came to see me only a few years ago. Seeing him was like being carried back to the happiest years of my life, and beyond the few clouds that have come between me and the sunlight, since I left Washington. What a bright, cheerful man Mr. Cameron is. If I were a man I

should want to be just as brisk and happy at eighty
as he is. He will never grow old. I always had a
great regard for him. It is a wonder how he retains
his health and great political power."

The following pen-portrait is from a correspondent
of the " Cincinnati Enquirer: " —

" It is comparatively easy to describe the bloom and
brilliancy of youth, but to draw with a true touch the peculiar loveliness of old age is a far more difficult task. A
woman like Mrs. Polk is a revelation of the beauties of old
age.   Gentle benevolence, broad-reaching charity, ripe
experience, and a cultivation of mind that extends beyond
letters to mankind, shine through her conversation, and a
ready memory, keen wit, and a store of reminiscences
illumine it. Sixty years ago, at the time of her marriage,
Mrs. Polk was considered remarkable for her beauty ; and
twenty years after, when she presided at the White House,
it was so fresh as to attract great admiration. Time has
stolen the vivid coloring and curved outlines of youth, but
he has not robbed her of the dignified carriage, and has
left brightness in her eyes and vivacity in her voice.
Crowned with eighty years of honor, she rose to receive
us, and I am not ashamed to say that something like dim-
ness came over my eyes at the sight of this brave widow,
who for nearly half a century has lived happy in the
thought that every day as it passes brings her one nearer
to her beloved husband. She has never accepted an invitation since her husband's death, though with graceful hospitality she has received each year the Tennessee legislature,
which adjourns in a body to call upon her, and which, I am
told, is the highest compliment ever paid by State authori-

ties to a lady ; and the civic, judicial, and ecclesiastical
bodies make it a point to pay their respects to her. Above
the sofa on which she sat hung a fine oil portrait of Mr.
Polk, for which he sat during his administration ; and near
it was one of herself, taken lately. In it she is dressed as
on the day I saw her, but until the picture caught my eye,
I had not noticed what she wore, — the greatest compliment
perfect taste can command. For a lady of her age and
position, nothing could be more fitting than the simple
black dress with its soft lace about the throat, and the close
widow's cap with its snowy border and graceful veil of
black tulle. Near at hand was a finely polished cane, and
at the head was tied a double bow of thick old-gold ribbon.
Among other things she referred to was the recent death of
Dr. Gross. ' It was only two years ago that he called upon
me,' she said, ' and we spent a most pleasant hour in talking
over old times, and he recalled with much animation a
party we both attended fifty years ago, and he even insisted
he remembered the very conversation he had with me. He
was a great man, and the news of his death pained me
deeply. Then, too, he was one of the few contemporaries
left me.' In bidding farewell, I expressed the hope that
her life would continue to flow on as pleasantly as now.
' Ah,' she answered, with a smile like soft sunlight, ' I cannot be here much longer, but I am quite willing to stay or
to go, whichever is best. My life has been very full, and
my friends very devoted. I have nothing to ask for, and
much to look forward to.' As we drove off, I silently won-
dered if any woman could see that dignified and charming
widow without the hope that she, too, might master the art
of growing old gracefully."

Governor Crittenden, of Missouri, with a large
party of gentlemen, called on Mrs. Polk, and was

received in the most gracious manner. He said in the " St. Louis Globe-Democrat: " —

" She takes deep concern in every movement in the interest of the South, and desires to see it prosperous and in harmony with the progressive views of all the States. Her home is always a charming visiting place for the old and young at Nashville, and for the thousands of strangers who go to that city. She is a devoted Christian, ever having a word of cheer for the prosperous, and of consoling sympathy for those whose lives have not fallen in such pleasant places. Her life will go out as gently and sweetly ' as dies the wave along the shore.' "

The following conversation was had with Mrs. Polk by a member of the " Nashville Banner " staff, and reported in that paper. Speaking of the Presidential election of 1844 as compared with that of 1884, she said : —

" So many years have elapsed since that event that the facts have almost faded from my memory ; and being the wife of one of the parties most interested, the excitement was kept far away from me. At that time our home was in Columbia, a small village, and we had no railroads and no telegraphic system."

" What were the questions then agitated ? Do you remember ? "

" Oh, yes. The question, then, as now, was largely about the tariff. In that particular, the two canvasses, forty years apart, are very similar. Another point of similarity was that without the vote of New York, Mr. Polk could not have been elected, and we were naturally very anxious to hear from that State. The ticket was ' Polk and Dallas,' and the battle-cry was 'Polk, Dallas, and Texas.' "

" Texas ? "

" Yes, the acquisition of Texas was another issue of the canvass. Of course, there were some opposed to it ; there is always somebody opposed to everything. There was never another canvass, save perhaps that immediately preceding the war, that equalled it in fervor."

" Was there more excitement than at the present time ? "

" All the information I have of the present canvass is what I glean from the newspapers and from what my friends tell me, and I judge that the feeling now is as a calm May morning to the turbulent, restless storm of excitement in those days. Every district had its political military company of organized troops, which if seen now would alarm the people to the verge of madness. Since the candidacy of Mr. Buchanan the canvass has always been too one-sided to create any excitement, except when Mr. Tilden and Mr. Hendricks were candidates, and perhaps now. My increasing age has toned down my ardor in such matters, though I always take a deep interest in State and national affairs. Even then it was necessary to the success of the ticket to carry New York. Pennsylvania was secured by the nomination of Mr. George M. Dallas for Vice-President, and he carried his own State. I regard the acquisition of Texas, and the results following the Mexican war, that is, the adding of California and New Mexico to the territory of the United States, as among the most important events in the history of this country, and that fact is becoming more and more apparent."

" Was the tariff the leading question in that canvass ? "

" That was one of the questions ; a tariff for revenue only was what the Democrats desired, while the Whigs contended that the higher the tariff the cheaper the goods. Another question was concerning United States banks, which it was desired to dispense with in favor of State banks."

A large party of editors of the New England Press Association, spent two days in Nashville in the course of their Southern tour. The " Lowell Citizen," the next month, published the following paragraphs descriptive of their visit : —

" Our party must needs pay their respects to the woman of whom Nashville is most proud, the venerable and venerated widow of President Polk. The broad mansion, with broad piazzas and stately columns, stands in the midst of more modern, but less home-like residences, in the heart of the city. A simple tomb of white marble breaks the green of the long lawn. Within the house we are received by ladies representing three generations of the family, Mrs. Polk herself, queenly in her dignity, and crowned with the chaplet of the highest womanhood ; Mrs. Fall, her niece ; and Miss Fall, her grand-niece. Our visit was but one of many such constantly being received by her, from all of which the visitors depart with a renewal of their natural belief in, and honor for, the gentle influence of the sex she so nobly represents.

" The Rev. Mr. Hatch, of the ' Hartford Courant,' thus addressed Mrs. Polk in behalf of the Association : ' Honored and venerated woman : The fame of your distinguished hospitality having reached our ears, we have ventured to visit your home and offer to you the tribute of our esteem. We honor you for the famous name you bear, and we ad-

mire the character that has added new lustre to the name.
We are a company of New England editors. Were we
ignorant of your eminent place in our country's history, we
should be unworthy the responsible position we hold. But
we do know and admire. When we remember your position in the chief home of this nation, and the dignified and
graceful bearing which has characterized your life here in
all these years, we are constrained to think of you not only
with the esteem of patriots, but also with the tender love of
sons.

> " ' Happy he
> With such a mother ! Faith in womankind
> Beats with his blood, and trust in all things high
> Comes easy to him.'

" ' We bid you adieu. God keep you. God bless you.' "

STILL BELOVED AND HONORED.

CHAPTER XIII.

1884–1891.

WHEN the Phi Delta Theta Society assembled in convention at Nashville the members called on Mrs. Polk, who was greatly pleased to meet so many young men, and to wish them all honor, happiness, and prosperity. They sang for her some of their lively fraternity songs.

Soon after, the delegates to the meeting of the National Grange and Patrons of Industry visited Polk Place in a body, and spent a pleasant hour there.

During a short stay in Nashville the Hon. Samuel J. Randall, with his wife called on Mrs. Polk. "The Banner" gave an account of this visit : —-

"Mr. Randall said that it afforded Mrs. Randall and himself a great pleasure thus to meet face to face the widow of the statesman and patriot and well-beloved President, James K. Polk. She replied that it was an equal pleasure to have the privilege of knowing one of the foremost men of the times, and the worthy successor to her own lamented husband. She expressed regret that Mr. Randall did not now occupy the Speaker's chair; adding that the responsibility and influence of the Speaker of the House was second only to that of the President himself. 'Indeed,' she warmly said, 'the Speaker, if the proper person, and with a correct idea of his position, has even more power and influence over legislation, and in directing the policy of parties, than the President or any other public officer.' Mr. Randall earnestly replied that the Speaker's place was indeed a most responsible one, and a position of such dignity and honor that it raises a man above the possibility of doing wrong, inspiring him with high thoughts and broad views. He reminded her of the fact that her husband was the only Speaker of the House of Representatives that was ever elected President of the United States."

In a party of business men from New York, was the Rev. Dr. Henry M. Field, in whose delightful conversation Mrs. Polk was much interested. She was especially pleased with the remark: "Madame, when I was travelling in Europe, during the Presidency of your husband, a letter of introduction written for me by him, gave me entrance into every house that I wished to visit." Mr. Inman represented the party in an address to Mrs. Polk, and was answered in her behalf by Mr. Thomas, President of the Nashville, Chattanooga, and St. Louis Railway Company.

While on a visit to Nashville Senator John Sherman spent an hour in conversation with Mrs. Polk, and the interview was much enjoyed by them both. He said that though she probably did not remember seeing him, long ago, he had a most happy remembrance of her, having called on her at the White House forty years before, during his bridal tour.

Early in 1887 Col. J. George Harris received a letter from his old friend, Mr. George Bancroft, announcing his intention of paying a visit to Mrs. Polk. The Tennessee Historical Society appointed their President, Judge Lea, with several others, as a committee to receive the historian. He arrived at seven o'clock on the evening of April 16th, accompanied by his German valet, Hermann, and was as spirited, active, and keenly observant as though he did not bear the burdens of nearly eighty-six years. He retired to his room at the Maxwell House, after taking a light refreshment; but soon after nine o'clock, apparently unfatigued by the long journey, went out with his valet for a walk. Mr. S. A. Cunningham meeting him on Vine Street, conducted him to Polk Place. The housekeeper opened the door in response to Hermann's touch of the bell, and Mr. Bancroft enquired cautiously if Mrs. Polk was still in the parlor. Hearing his voice, she at once appeared in the doorway, when he sprang forward with an enthusiastic salutation: "Dear Mrs. Polk, I am so glad to see you looking so very well."

"I am grateful to you, Mr. Bancroft, for coming so far to see us."

These two belong so emphatically to the scenes of a completed past, that this meeting in familiar converse suggests two stately figures in an historic picture stepping from the frame to talk over the life of the olden time. The next day was Sunday and Mr. Bancroft occupied Mrs. Polk's pew in church, although she was unable to be present. He dined with her, and in the quiet and freedom of this hour of home comfort and refreshment, the two old friends recalled many pleasing incidents of the past.

The well-known banker and philanthropist, Mr. Corcoran, had sent her a letter by the hand of his friend: —

MY DEAR MADAME, — I have just learned from my friend and neighbor, Mr. Bancroft, that he intends to go to-morrow to Nashville, on purpose to see you, and I avail myself of the opportunity to send to you and your sweet niece my best regards and homage. Wishing you all health and happiness, sincerely yours,

W. W. CORCORAN.

On Monday afternoon Mrs. Polk and Mr. Bancroft received the many friends who came to express their esteem and regard for the venerable hostess and her distinguished friend. The subdued hum of conversation, the soft strains of the music, the mild light of the wax candles in the chandeliers, and the presence of Mr. Bancroft, no doubt brought forcibly to the mind of Mrs. Polk the far-off Washington days. The next morning's " American " said : —

"The two venerable and historic personages at first stood together at the south end of the room ; the lady however, soon took an arm-chair near by, but Mr. Bancroft remained standing throughout the reception. His eye was bright, his form erect, his conversation quick, his sympathy responsive, his manner genial. The gathering included many from neighboring towns, and many of Nashville's best citizens."

One object of Mr. Bancroft's visit was to gather from the papers of Mr. Polk certain materials for his historical work. He made a partial examination of the manuscripts, but many pressing invitations allowed him little leisure for his task, and Mrs. Polk consented to send to him at Washington a trunk filled with these important documents. Several months after his return home, the papers were all copied and bound, ready for reference, and the originals were returned to Nashville.

14

A committee representing the Tennessee Historical Society escorted Mr. Bancroft, on the following Tuesday, to the Nashville University, now the Normal College. Entering the beautiful grounds, Judge Lea pointed to a cluster of eleven trees that he had planted in memory of his fellow-graduates in the class of 1837, mentioning after a pause, that he was the only one then left. The Central Tennessee College, and Fisk University, both for colored students, received Mr. Bancroft with outbursts of song, the organ and orchestra mingling with the wild, yet sweet music of hundreds of negro voices. At the Fisk, Mr. Bancroft concluded his words to the students with this sentence: "Lift up your hearts; rise in the dignity of your souls."

In the evening, the rooms of the Historical Society, filled with relics and curiosities, and decorated with historic portraits, were thrown open in honor of the great historian. He enjoyed the social greetings so thoroughly that formal introductions were not attempted. Judge Lea stated that Mr. Bancroft had long been an honorary member of the Society. He referred to the important part Mr. Bancroft had taken in the administration of the Government, and to the high place he had assumed and worthily held, through fifty years, as the historian of this western world. In recalling some scenes

connected with our revolutionary struggle, Judge
Lea said that many writers had treated the battle of
King's Mountain as only a successful skirmish,
while Mr. Bancroft had shown it to have been a
decisive battle, one of the turning-points of the
Revolution. Then addressing Mr. Bancroft, he
continued, " You speak of it as having changed
the aspect of the war, as inspiring the soldiers like
the ringing cry of Concord, as being in its effects
like the success at Bennington. This is a tribute
to the people who afterward organized the State of
Tennessee. Honorable mention, too, you make of
the pioneers of the Watauga settlement, and a clear
statement is given of the Scotch-Irish who sought
homes in the western country, the chief of whom,
General James Robertson, the founder of Nashville,
whose portrait is just opposite this platform, you
characterize as possessed of a true nobleness of
soul, intrepid and patriotic. It is natural, therefore,
that the people of Nashville should recognize an
obligation greater perhaps than you are aware, and
the visit of no distinguished citizen could have been
to them more acceptable."

In response, Mr. Bancroft said he was glad that
the President of the Society had spoken of him as a
member. " I stand here to-night," he went on, " as
a friend and a brother. Tennessee can well afford

to have an historical society.   Men of highest moral character were the pioneers of this section.   I am amazed at your wealth and culture.   The immigrants who came here brought the purest principles, and the men of Tennessee have exerted an influence on the habits of men not only in this country, but throughout the world.   Who was it that said, ' The Union; it must and shall be preserved'?   He was your fellow-citizen.   The world has not yet given all the honor that is in store for Andrew Jackson. He will live in sweetest affection.   I knew him well, and look on him as second only to George Washington.   Nor need we name him alone.   I remember with pride the achievements of Polk's administration.   I can testify to the wonderful capacity of his mind."   With proud emphasis he added, " We are one.   May our Union be founded on a rock.   I have always turned to the South with a pride in her integrity and patriotism, no less than to the North. The results of our solidified Union are showing themselves in Europe, and will in Asia, and throughout the world."

Mr. Bancroft's last morning in the city was spent in visiting Belle Meade, five miles away, looking at the fine blooded horses, and enjoying the rare sight of the herd of beautiful deer, roving in the park.

Among the many newspaper comments on this

notable visit, we quote only the following from the " St. Louis Republican : " —

" The meeting between the estimable lady who has been an ex-President's widow for thirty-eight years, and the venerable old gentleman who was first her husband's Secretary of the Navy, and afterward his minister to the Court of St. James, was most courtly, cordial, and happy. The days of the Polk administration were an age of courtly grace and sentiment, and in its mellow splendor neither of them dreamed of the tragic four years with the following era of hard materialism which they have lived to see. Mr. Bancroft is well on toward ninety, and Mrs. Polk is close behind him."

In October Mr. and Mrs. Cleveland visited Nashville, and were guests of General Jackson at Belle Meade. They arrived on Saturday night, and wishing to give Mrs. Polk due precedence and attention by seeing her before the public reception on Monday morning, they called on her on Sunday afternoon, desiring to make a quiet, informal visit. The Harding turnpike was thronged with the vehicles of those who were anxious to get a glimpse of the President and his wife as they drove into the city; and the streets around Polk Place were filled with a similarly expectant crowd, who doffed their hats and cheered, as the President's carriage drove rapidly by. Mr. Fall met the party at the steps of

the portico, and bade them welcome. Mrs. Polk
and the President enjoyed a free and animated talk
about Washington and the Executive Mansion;
and referring to this conversation afterward, she
said, " During our talk we built and rebuilt the
White House." After refreshments had been served,
the guests went to look at the tomb. Soon afterward farewells were said, and Mrs. Polk, leaning
upon the arm of ex-Governor Porter, went to the
steps of the portico to see the party leave. The
President took off his hat to the company at the
door, his wife bowed good-by, and the carriage was
quickly driven away, followed by the cheers of the
assembled crowds. This visit was unique. It
brought together for a brief social meeting two
ladies, the elder of whom entered the White House
as mistress in 1845, and the younger in 1885, just
forty years afterward, a circumstance never occur-
ring before and not likely to occur again.

In November, before the assembling of the National Convention of the Woman's Christian Tem-
perance Union in Nashville, their President, Miss
Willard, paid a brief visit to Polk Place. It was
pleasant to see in simple, familiar converse these
two women, the one in middle life having already
attained a world-wide reputation by her work with
voice and pen, and the other venerable in years and

honors, holding as she had done for half a century the unfeigned affection of the American people. The two sat in a *tête-à-tête* armchair with reverse seats, so that they were *vis-à-vis* as well as side by side. Mrs. Polk remarking that she could write a letter as easily after dinner as in the forenoon, Miss Willard said playfully that she was going to tell her mother, who was eighty-three years old and accustomed to write only in the fresh morning hours, that Mrs. Polk said it made no difference, and so she might write in the afternoon also. The ebony cane mounted with a silver hand-rest which Miss Fall had brought from London for her aunt, was Miss Willard's special admiration and referring again to her mother, she said that she had arranged hand-rests, little crutches she called them, in various parts of the house, at the head and foot of the stair-ways, and on the landings, wherever her mother might need help in walking.

About a hundred members of the convention called one day at the noon hour, and were introduced to Mrs. Polk. Many other members of the Union visited Polk Place, in groups, at odd times. A delegate from New York had brought her baby to the Convention. She called upon Mrs. Polk, and said, waving her hand toward the baby in the nurse's arms, "Madame, you have seen the eldest member of the W. C. T. U. Convention; this is the youngest." These visits were enjoyed by the aged hostess. "If I were younger," she said, "I would certainly attend your meetings." Her unqualified admiration was excited by the undreamed-of powers developed in woman by the novel circumstances of modern times.

Among her visitors, soon afterward, was the sculptor Valentine, of Richmond, who had just come from the unveiling of his bronze statue of John Cabell Breckinridge, at Lexington, Kentucky. The evangelist Sayford, of Boston, with his quartette, also called; as did Thomas Nelson Page, who had been entertaining large audiences with recitations from his stories of Southern life in that old régime now fast receding into the past. She said to Mr. Page that the friends she had known many years ago, in Richmond, were all dead, and that it was very kind in him to call on one who was but a relic of the past. To which he replied, " Madame, you have as many friends in Richmond now as you had in the olden times." This rejoinder awakened in her heart the feeling of gratitude which was so often heard from her lips; and she said: "I am astonished at so much attention being paid me, an old woman on the verge of the grave. I recognize nothing in myself;

I am only an atom in the hands of God, who does it all." She added, " My husband lived in distinguished times, and all these honors I take as being done for his sake, for he is better understood now than in those days."

In the April following Mrs. Polk sent a telegram of inquiry as to Mr. Bancroft's health, and received this message in response: —

I am in most excellent health; splendid appetite, seven hours unbroken sleep at night; and, thank God, I have good friends like you to comfort me.

GEORGE BANCROFT.

Mrs. Hayes, of Baltimore, the venerable President of the Woman's Missionary Societies of the Methodist Church, spent a quiet hour with Mrs. Polk. She had reached her seventy-fifth year the day before, and it was pleasant to them both to recall the friends and incidents of the half-century just passed.

About this time Miss Ballentine, Principal of the young women's department of Fisk University, made herself known to Mrs. Polk as the daughter of the Rev. E. Ballentine, pastor of the Presbyterian Church at Washington at the time when President Polk and his wife worshipped there. She received

the daughter of her former pastor with evident
pleasure, and with many recollections of her father's
ministrations. On the eve of Mr. Polk's retirement from office Mr. Ballentine had presented
to him and his wife a copy of the Bible, and
also of " The Pilgrim's Progress." The Bible she
now gave to his daughter, in affectionate remembrance of her father, knowing that no one else
would so prize a keepsake which had been carefully preserved for nearly forty years. Miss Ballentine said that it should be a precious heir-loom
in her family, and would now be given to the
youngest son of her youngest brother, a child
two years old, who bears the name of his grandfather. On the flyleaf of each had been written
a letter of presentation in which the pastor begs
the President and his wife to accept the books
" as proofs of his high regard, and of his earnest
wishes for their temporal and eternal welfare.
May the Bible be their Counsellor and Comforter,
and the Progress of the Pilgrim to Zion theirs
during their earthly lives. February 24th, 1849."

It was less than four months after he had left
Washington, that the astonishing tidings of Mr.
Polk's death flashed over the country; and on
the 24th of June, Mr. Ballentine preached a
memorial sermon, exactly four months from the

date of his inscription in the Bible. An extract
from this discourse may be quoted : —

"That last Sabbath of his attendance in this
sanctuary has by his death become invested with
new and affecting interest. It was the 4th of
March, the last day of his Presidency. His term
of office commenced with a solemn oath in the
name of his Maker, and closed while he was
engaged with us in the services of God's worship,
— certainly a sacred, solemn moment, when the
holy employment might stimulate the sense of
accountability, and the desire of God's accept-
ance, and excite to prayer in behalf of the country
he loved, whose government he had administered
with so much assiduity, energy, and ability. We
remember with sad interest now his retiring at
the close of the services, from the seat he had
so long occupied, and how he gave the parting
hand to those around him. It was not without
deep emotion that he said to an elder of the
church, whom he met among the last in the aisle,
as he shook his hand and called him by name, 'I
shall never worship with you again.' A predic-
tion how soon and sadly confirmed. To her whom
this sudden stroke has deprived of the desire of
her eyes, who so long and so lately had a
place in our sanctuary, the savor of whose Chris-

tian character was as ointment poured forth in the exalted place she occupied, to her we tender our Christian sympathy, and we pray that, according to the rich and sure promises of the Bible, God may be her God both now and forever."

On one occasion the writers met at Polk Place the daughter of Mr. Polk's sister Ophelia, now Mrs. Naomi Hayes Moore, and her daughter Ophelia. Her husband, Major W. E. Moore, was chief commissary of the Army of the Tennessee. She had shared with him the hardships of war, early in the sixties, and this exposure brought on a throat affection, resulting in irremediable deafness. Her bright, eager eyes, scarching in the faces of those around her for intelligible signs of the thoughts flowing from their lips, showed her mental vivacity. The daughter, a living illustration of filial devotion, busily employed her fair hands in the graceful finger-language, telling her mother what was said, and enabling her to take a part in the conversation. In the awful railroad accident which occurred near Statesville, North Carolina, in August, 1891, Miss Ophelia Moore was killed. A few days afterward, a small gold watch was found in the wreck. Engraved on the back is the coat of arms of the Polk family, — a wild boar pierced through, and four bugles, with the motto, "audacter et strenue."

The 4th of July, 1888, was the opening day of the Cincinnati Centennial Exposition, commemorating the progress of Ohio and the Central States during the century. Mrs. Polk, as the eldest widow of an ex-President, was chosen to touch the electric button, which was to give the signal to set the vast machinery in motion. Telegraph wires were carried into her residence, and the instruments placed upon the marble table sent from Tunis in 1849. A score or more of gentlemen were present as invited guests. Mr. J. U. Rust and Mr. A. H. Stewart manipulated the wires for the Western Union Telegraph Company. At a quarter past eleven o'clock, the following telegram was received: —

CENTENNIAL HALL, CINCINNATI, July 4, 1888.

GREETING TO MRS. JAMES K. POLK: That upon this auspicious moment, when heaven has smiled upon this glorious northwestern territory, the same beneficent providence has spared to the citizens of the United States the wife of their revered President, James K. Polk.

JAMES ALLISON, *President.*

The Rev. Dr. Witherspoon was requested to read the message to the deeply interested group round the table. She replied immediately, as follows:

" Mrs. Polk acknowledges the courteous telegram just received, and hereby returns her thanks for the kind remembrance of her husband and herself upon this memorable occasion."

There is a difference of twenty-two minutes between the two cities, Nashville going by standard time, and Cincinnati preferring sun-time; and at thirty-eight minutes past eleven o'clock here, it was twelve o'clock there.   At this moment Mrs. Polk pressed the key, in response to which came this dispatch : —

" When Mrs. Polk touched the key the machinery started, bells rang, hundreds of electric lights flashed out, and the entire concourse of people rose and cheered amid the waving of flags and banners. Such a thrilling scene has not been witnessed for years."

An outburst of applause from the little audience in Polk Place greeted the reading of this message, and the only quiet person in the assembly was the venerable lady who was the centre of observation. A gentleman standing near bowed to her and said, " We are not going to let you go down, Mrs. Polk. We will keep you up by electricity, if by nothing else."   She received many congratulations, and replied to them in the manner peculiar to herself. To Dr. Witherspoon she said, " The honor which has been paid me does not appeal to my pride. I recognize that it is a compliment to Mr. Polk, and it is one which I appreciate fully. Such tokens of remembrance of my husband, expressed through kindness to me, have cheered me all along to the very evening of life, and I am deeply grateful for them."

The " American " thus concludes a long account of this unique event : —

"The honor paid to Mrs. Polk was an honor to the womanhood of the South, whose virtues this venerable lady embodies, and as such will not easily be forgotten."

During the following year she was much pleased by the visit of a group of New York capitalists, among whom were Abram S. Hewitt, Edward Cooper, a son of Peter Cooper, and John C. Calhoun, a descendant of the distinguished statesman whose full name he bears. Mrs. Polk had been intimately associated with Mr. Calhoun's grandparents on both sides. The stream of reminiscence awakened by the surprise and pleasure of seeing him made her unusually bright and cheerful. She also enjoyed the conversation with Mr. Hewitt, enriched by his overflowing fund of information concerning things past as well as present. " He knows everything," she said.

When the Rev. Dr. H. M. Field passed through Nashville, on his return from a long sojourn in Florida, she sent special regards to Mr. Bancroft, as Dr. Field intended staying several days in Washington. Some time afterward, the following letter came to her: —

" MY DEAR MRS. POLK, — Yesterday afternoon, in company with my brother, Judge Field, I paid a visit to Mr. Bancroft. We found him in his library, looking somewhat aged, but still bright with all his old fire. He was delighted to see us, and especially gratified to receive the message from you, to which he replied in the warmest manner, saying that no one since Mrs. Washington had filled the place you occupied here with more perfect grace and dignity, and that you were remembered by the older residents with the utmost respect and affection. Nor was he less ardent in his praise of your husband, whose administration he pronounced one of the most brilliant in American history. This great distinction, he said, was due to Mr. Polk himself; that he was not, like some Presidents, a mere figure-head of the Government, to be ruled by his Cabinet, but that, while he had indeed a Cabinet which comprised men of great ability, yet that he was the ablest of them all. He spoke of the great events of his administration, — the Mexican war, the acquisition of Texas and of California, the latter bringing with it the great empire on the Pacific coast. All this was very high praise, to come from the historian of our country. After an hour's visit we could hardly tear ourselves from the eloquent old man, and as we parted he begged us to send to Mrs. Polk his most affectionate remembrance. To this I may add my own, and beg that you will now and then give a thought to one who considers it an honor to be permitted to call himself your friend."

In a letter to a correspondent in Nashville, Dr. Field said: —

"Will you present my regards especially to Mrs. Polk? I wish you could have heard Mr. Bancroft speak of her, and of her honored husband. Please tell her that I mean to come to Nashville again, if it were only to pay my respects to her. How truly she finds that ' at evening time it shall be light.' So may it be until this soft beautiful twilight fades into the light of heaven."

Healy's portrait of Mr. Polk was copied for his niece, Mrs. Barnett, by Miss Zollicoffer of Columbia. This portrait occupied a prominent place in the large tent in which the Scotch-Irish Congress held

their proceedings in that city in May, 1889. Upon
his return from this convention, Colonel McClure
of Philadelphia, with his wife and their party, called
upon Mrs. Polk. Referring to his visit of several
years before, he said that after leaving the mansion
he felt ashamed that he had remained so long. So
engrossed was he in the conversation that he was
beguiled into a longer stay than he had intended.

A company of librarians from the New England
States came during this month, and a brief eloquent
address was made to her by Mr. Justin Winsor,
Librarian of Harvard College. At its close he and
his companions made a bow in unison, the grace
and heartiness of which impressed her very pleasantly. In the same month a number of Ohio editors, passing through Nashville, paid their respects
to her. One of this company, Mr. Lewis Green,
wrote thus of the visit: "At eleven o'clock, our
party called upon Mrs. Polk. Her welcome was
hearty and gracious, and she had a smile and a
kind word for all. Probably no company ever
invaded the parlors of the old mansion, that was
better pleased with their reception than ours."

During the meeting of the American Medical
Association a large number of physicians, with
their wives and friends, called on her. As they
were presented, instinctively a hand now and then

was offered, but was quickly and courteously put
back by the cautious master of ceremonies; for the
cordial custom of hand-shaking was too fatiguing to
the cheery but feeble octogenarian. The next day,
when she had a visit from a smaller number of
medical men, not present at the former call, a tall,
spare, gray-haired Pennsylvanian bent over, and
seizing her hand, held it while he poured forth a
torrent of eloquence, tears streaming down his
cheeks, and as he closed, pressing his lips to her
hand. The others looked on in respectful silence.
His emotion made a deep impression not only on
Mrs. Polk, but on all present.

On one occasion an ex-governor of Massachusetts pleased her greatly by the praise he bestowed upon her husband, and the important acts
of his administration. He also said that he had
been very desirous of seeing a former resident of
the White House about whom no unkind criticism
or complaint had ever been made. She enjoyed
the interview, but smilingly told him that had he
not been accompanied by her relative, Mr. Childress, he would not have gained an admittance, as
her feebleness often prevented her meeting visitors.
In receiving the Rev. Mr. Miller of Princeton, New
Jersey, she said she was so weak that it was only
the "Rev." before his name that induced her to

see him. He commended her faithfulness to Presbyterian principles, — a faithfulness without merit,
she thought, as it was a part of the warp and woof
of her nature, a part of the heritage of her fathers.

Professor Bourland, of the Peabody Normal
School, escorted about fifty of the pupils to Polk
Place. They represented several southern States.
As she looked at them she thought: " This is a free
school, and who knows but that some young person now present who has been helped by kind
friends to come here and get an education may
some day rise to power and exert a wide influence
for good?" " This visit was very agreeable to me,"
she afterward said; then raising her palm-leaf fan to
her face, and laughing quietly, added, " but if they
had been old politicians — ! "

A young man from North Carolina told her that
his father was a Democrat, and had worked hard for
Mr. Polk in 1844, and that he had requested him
to see Mrs. Polk, if possible, and to convey to her
his respectful remembrances. She assured him, as
she had often before assured college students who
wished to ask questions concerning her husband,
that it made her happy to talk about him. One of
the students was a young man of fine proportions,
who had been engaged in some occupation on a
steamboat, until his desire for the profession of a

teacher led him to the Normal School. His enthusiasm was aroused by the interview, and he exclaimed when they had left her presence, " I never
felt so much like being good and doing good as
when I saw her."

HOME SCENES AND INCIDENTS.

MRS. POLK.

Copy of Drury's portrait, painted in 1878.

CHAPTER XIV.

1881–1885.

THE guests assembled at " Our Home on the Hillside," a summer resort at Dansville, New York, were talking one day on the engrossing theme of President Garfield's illness, and discussing the latest bulletin in the morning newspaper. Recalling various incidents connected with the White House, some one remembered that it contained no portrait of Mrs. President Polk. After an animated interchange of opinion on the subject, Miss Frances Willard suggested that the present occasion was a fitting time to set on foot an effort to secure the desired portrait. Suitable resolutions were adopted and a committee composed of representative women chosen, and empowered to carry out the details of the plan. The order was given to Mr. Dury of Nashville. In due time Mrs. Porter, the President of the Ladies' Association at Nashville, received a letter from Senator Jackson in which he announced the arrival of the portrait at Washington, and its conveyance by himself and his colleague, Senator Harris, to the Executive Mansion, where it was to be hung in a place to be designated by President Arthur. This picture was a copy of Healy's portrait, taken when Mrs. Polk was mistress of the White House. In 1878, when she was seventy-five years old, she had sat to Mr. Dury for her portrait, and the artist has well preserved her familiar features and bright expression.

Her home, year after year, grew richer in pictures and rare objects. In the large hall near an engraving of the Washington Monument, and of the equestrian statue of General Jackson, hung a portrait of Mr. Polk, painted by Healy for Judge Catron. After the death of the Judge and his wife it had been presented to Mrs. Fall by Mrs. Jane Marshall, who thought Polk Place the safest depository for so valuable a picture. In the dining-room were two attractive old portraits: one of Mrs. Childress, Mrs. Polk's mother; the other of Mrs. Jetton, Mrs. Fall's mother. In the east parlor was a portrait of Mr. Polk by a Nashville artist, Mr. William Cooper; while another by his brother, Mr. Washington B. Cooper, hung over the mantel-piece in Mrs. Polk's bedroom. In this homelike chamber was the massive furniture of former days. An immense four-post canopied bedstead occupied a large space. Here upon a centre-table stood a student's lamp; and the books, papers, pen, and ink, were arranged in the order which betokened a habit of carefulness. This room was shared with the little niece Saidee, when a child.

The relics, heirlooms and treasures with which the house abounded, were assigned to one and another of her friends, to be delivered after her death. Of this nearing event she always spoke with as much quietness as she would of taking an ordinary journey. To Saidee, the pet of the household, the greater part of these mementos has fallen. Among them is a trunk full of the Paris dresses worn by the President's wife on state occasions. Other treasures were the heavy gold watch, the spectacles, pencil-case, and pen used by her husband. She kept these with the inauguration Bible in a box fashioned of dark wood ornamented with a band of bird's-eye maple, covered with a glass lid, and fastened with a tiny lock and key. Red tissue-paper and masses of white cotton concealed the Bible and other reminders of pleasant occupations in the past. This watch had belonged to an elder brother of Mr. Polk's, a handsome, dashing young man, who one day took it from his pocket, and placed it in that of his brother, saying that his brother's watch was too plain. This brother was not twenty-five years old when he died, away from home; and one of his last messages was that his brother James should have the watch. After Mr. Polk's death it was worn by his brother William; and when he died, it was sent to Mrs. Polk. Some years before her own death she sent it to Tasker, a son of William H. Polk, of North Carolina.

During the war Major William H. Polk and the Hon. Bailie Peyton, of Tennessee, went to Washington, to confer with the Government concerning an exchange of prisoners. While they were there, an officer in the Federal army, whose name is now forgotten, gave to Major Polk a watch that he said had once belonged to General Washington, and afterward to General Robert E. Lee. Engraved on the back was the letter W. Returning to Columbia, Major Polk handed it to his wife, requesting her, in the event of his death before the end of the war, to see that it was returned to General Lee, or his family. After his death, not willing to risk so valuable a relic in a passage through the army from Tennessee to North Carolina, she took it to Mrs. Polk, asking her to return it to General Lee. Immediately after the surrender Mrs. William H. Polk wrote to General Lee concerning the watch. He replied that if it came from the White House, Virginia, or from Arlington, it was his property; if not, it did not belong to him. Mrs. Polk sent it on, and as it proved to be his, received from him a courteous letter of thanks.

Early in 1882 a bill appropriating a pension to the venerable widow of ex-President Polk was introduced in Congress, and ably advocated by Senator Jackson and his colleague. In the House of Representatives the Tennessee delegation successfully urged its passage. It was amended so as to include all the widows of former Presidents, then living; and the pension was fixed at five thousand dollars per annum. The justice of such an appropriation may be better understood, in Mrs. Polk's case, by referring to an address made by ex-Governor Aaron V. Brown in the Democratic Convention, in January, 1852, in the Capitol at Nashville. Speaking of Mr. Polk, he said, " From yonder window you may look out on the spot where lies entombed all that was mortal of that eminent and good man. But if you would contemplate the never-dying principles which he illustrated and adorned, you must extend your view far beyond our present horizon. You must gaze with amazement over the whole area of this great continent; on Texas now teeming with a contented population; on California and Oregon already building up cities on the distant shores of the Pacific, and opening for us the way to the boundless wealth and commerce of the Asiatic world. Never until we have taken a broad, national survey like this, shall we be prepared to pay homage to the great principles of Jackson and Polk."

In a familiar conversation on the pension, Mrs. Polk said, "I've often thought, if I had a strip of California I would make Sallie rich, — and you too," she added, looking at a friend sitting beside her. She helped many who came to the door, saying that a little money would at least give them bread; she preferred, however, to assist the needy through the Relief Society and similar associations, in order that the gift might be wisely dispensed. But, to use her own words, she " had no surplus to donate to institutions of learning or benevolence."

On Decoration Day, at the National Cemetery near Nashville, Colonel House of Indianapolis delivered an original poem. He visited Mrs. Polk while here, and after returning home, sent the following sonnet to the " Nashville American: "

SERUS IN COELUM REDEAS.

" Dear lady, when life's day was young and fair,
   Thine own and country's, then thy youthful eyes
   Caught glow of cloudless light from happy skies.
Though thou hast stood within their noontide glare,
   The fountains of thy heart were not dried bare ;
   Nor when arose dense clouds of funeral dyes,
   And hope afar seemed clothed in sombre guise,

Didst thou lose youthful heart or greet despair.
And as from thy calm eyes we catch the gleam
Of skies that once o'erarched life's flowery plain,
The phantom Time fades from us like a dream,
And comes the thought that, born 'neath fairy reign,
Thou found'st in days when ruled the old régime
The fountain Ponce de Leon sought in vain."

A few months after Mrs. Polk's marriage in January, 1824, one of her friends was visiting the home of Mr. John Catron, at Rokeby, not far from where the Vanderbilt University now stands. This friend told her that when Mr. Catron came home one evening, he said that he had been asked what sort of a girl James K. Polk had married, and that he had replied, " Oh, a poor, sickly thing, who will not live a year." He used to repeat this incident with much amusement long afterward, when time had proved that he was not so well fitted to be a judge of feminine longevity as of the intricate problems of the law. In her old age, when Judge Catron himself and all who had heard the remark were dead, she often spoke of the impressive fact that of all that circle of friends she alone was living.

On the 4th of September, 1883, she was eighty years old. A complete surprise was given her by the congratulations of many friends. Some scores of citizens, more or less prominent, paid their re-

spects. Mrs. Dr. Cheatham sent a large bouquet,
the figures "80" in the centre made of tuberoses
on an ample background of crimson geraniums,
the whole bordered with heliotropes and other delicate blossoms. Bouquets were also sent by several
others.

The newspapers on the following morning contained these lines: —

Sept. 4, 1803.   Sept. 4, 1883.

To the Hon. Mrs. James K. Polk.

The path of the just is as the shining light, that shineth
more and more unto the perfect day. — Proverbs iv. 18.

> The singers of the earth, with plaintive strain,
> That fills the soul with sense of loss and pain,
> Lament the course of life's declining day,
> That slowly, surely leads to evening gray,
> Just when high noon is glorious and complete,
> And strength and skill make every labor sweet.
>
> But are they not with partial view content?
> And, Madame, make they not undue lament?
> They see alone the body's sad decline,
> But think not of the spirit's essence fine,
> Which grows in wisdom and in beauty still,
> With each experience of good and ill.
>
> Thus, growing greater still, thy life appears,
> Seen through the vista of these eighty years;
> Beginning with the maiden's gentle ways,
> Compelling then the world's admiring gaze,
> And then, through sad bereavement's chastening power,
> Attaining character's most lovely flower.

Mid clustering memories of life's happy day,
Thou waitest gladly in its evening gray,
With eyes of faith turned westward to the sky,
Behind whose rainbow banners, towering high,
Stand Heaven's bright gates, which soon will open wide,
And thou wilt go where life and light abide.

F. D. N.

From an editorial of the " American," the same day, the following sentences are taken: —

" This country has produced no statesman whose home was happier than was that of the great man who sleeps so quietly while the beloved wife watches over his grave. Through all his conflicts, and as the tide of fortune carried him up, she was ever by his side. She is well preserved, exceedingly cheerful and bright, and is the highest type of a Christian woman."

One afternoon, in the middle of March, when we called to inquire after her health, and one spoke of the fresh, green leaves, and the yellow spring flowers, looking like spots of gold, and the purple and pink hyacinths on either side of the long walk, she said, " Are they blooming? The flowers and I are alike, both going downward." This was said with a smile, as if she concurred in the wisdom of nature, which made it necessary for her to fade and disappear. Like the flowers that had rejoiced in their free and fragrant life, so had she rejoiced in hers. As we rose to go, and spoke of the Immigration Committee guests of the city who had called

on her the week before, she said that she had received so many calls of respect and so many marks
of kindness that she feared she was not as appre-
ciative as she wished to be. "If, in my old age,"
she continued, "I can give pleasure to my fellow-
citizens by receiving them, it gives me pleasure to
do so." Then she resumed, smilingly, "You know
a woman never grows too old to be indifferent to
a compliment."

One day when the June heat brought to every one
a sense of lassitude she expressed a feeling of a loss
of interest in public as well as in private affairs, —
a loosening of the links binding her to the world of
thought and action. Some one remarked that probably the feeling was owing to a lessening of her
physical strength. A moment after, however, she
began to dwell with evident interest upon the merits
of the candidates for the presidency. And when
one of the group, changing the subject, mentioned
the recent elaborate celebration of the six hundredth
anniversary of the charming of the children of
Hamelin by the Pied Piper, she remarked with animation that, both in Europe and in America, much
more attention than formerly was now paid to
historical incidents, and to the gathering of data for
history and biography. Then with a little glow of
animation she continued: "The journals of the day

contain many interesting historical references, and it would be pleasant to read them if it were not for the flaming head-lines of dreadful deeds just committed that deface almost every column."

Admiring the striking and popular sermons of Dr. ——, she said that in the judgment of former days, his excellence would have been marred by his peculiarities. "How the times have changed!" she exclaimed; "but it is necessary for every one to advance with the times, so that the generation passing away may not be too widely separated from the one just arising. When our church was trying to find a suitable pastor," she continued, "some one asked me what my choice was. 'I have no choice to make,' I replied. 'What! consult an old lady about the selection of a minister? It is not to old ladies that the minister comes to preach. It is his chief calling to gather the young in, and to interest them that they may become Christians. I could sit at home, and read a sermon, and do very well. It is the young people who must be pleased in the choice of a minister.'"

The conversation drifting to the subject of religious newspapers, her opinion was that they draw us too much away from the Bible. The various beautiful lives of Christ, and the multitude of religious publications satisfied us, she thought, and consumed the hours that ought to be spent in reading chapter after chapter of the Divine Oracles.

Speaking one day of the religious movements of the time, mention was made of a recent series of meetings of ladies for Scripture-study and prayer, which had attracted much attention in the city. Miss G. had begun a little meeting of a few friends for prayer and Bible-study, which soon grew to large proportions, filling the double parlors of her father's house. Replying to a remark concerning this un- usual manifestation of interest in spiritual themes, Mrs. Polk said: "I have always believed in prayer, and I believe in it still. I told Miss G. that if I were younger and stronger, I too would go to her meetings. Let the ladies pray, and if they think any sickness they have may be cured by prayer, it is a beautiful faith. I have often prayed for such things, and whenever I have failed to get the desired answer, my faith was only strengthened, because I considered that my prayer might not have been made in the right spirit or at the right time, and that another time my desire might be granted."

Her mind reverting to the Rev. Mr. Henderson, who had officiated at her marriage, she said that in those old times he once preached a sermon in the Court House in Nashville, to the few Presbyte- rians living in the city, who had then no house of

public worship. He spoke strongly against duel-
ling, which in those days was a not infrequent occurrence, and enlarged upon its sin and evil con-
sequences. To the dismay of his friends, General
Jackson sat among the auditors, — whether known or
not to the preacher declaiming so earnestly against
one of his practices, they could not tell. He was
aware, however, that the general would certainly
hear of the sermon. The next morning, while the
good friends were still trembling for Mr. Henderson,
supposing that he had incurred the wrath of the
fiery soldier, the general had already visited a tailor
and ordered for the minister the finest suit of clothes
that could be made!

When any one presumed that the inquiries of
strangers concerning Mr. Polk's life would become
monotonous, or be deemed an intrusion upon the
sacredness of her gravest memories, she would
reply: " I feel an exquisite pleasure in giving information, especially to young men, concerning his
public and private life, for of course I deem it a life
eminently worthy of emulation. Not long ago, a
number of college students called upon me. In the
course of a most agreeable conversation I observed
that some of the young gentlemen hesitated to
make inquiries for certain information of a somewhat personal nature concerning Mr. Polk's life.

Anticipating their wishes, I told them that nothing delighted me more than to resurrect these long-ago facts, and thus contribute to the happiness of others."

She said that during Mr. Polk's lifetime she often had a delicacy in repeating compliments paid to him, but that now she did so without scruple. She had a natural reluctance to any conversation about her own experiences, and it was difficult to draw from her the information essential to a faithful story of her life.

Many letters came to her from strangers, making divers requests: that she would join a certain praise-worthy society; that she would contribute to this or that deserving object; that she would give items of information regarding some one she had known sixty years ago; that she would grant the favor of a few pieces for a crazy quilt, etc., etc. Every day or two brought applications for her autograph. Kindness and courtesy impelled her to comply with these appeals as far as possible, but in her later years many of them were, of necessity, indefinitely postponed. Until the last months of life her eyes were good, and she used them to her heart's content in the luxury of reading. She could still read large print with unaided sight, and would sometimes look over her letters, and pen one or two short

answers, before putting on her glasses; and would
often express a profound gratitude for the long-con-
tinued gift of strong and clear vision. While the
feebleness of advanced age made walking somewhat difficult, she was still animated in manner and
bright in conversation, showing the ready tact and
wit of former times. She was obliged to excuse
herself to many callers, but those who saw her
found her still so young and fresh in her interest
and sympathy that it seemed strange to hear her
speak of the impossibility of keeping up the correspondence and the social habits of other days. Her
interest in the newspapers was a never-failing source
of pleasure. Her insight into the hidden springs of
action and change in national and local affairs was
remarkable, when it is considered that for nearly
two-score years she had lived continuously in the
retirement of her quiet home.

REMINISCENCES.

CHAPTER XV.

1885–1891.

ONE day Mrs. Polk told us that in the first year of Mr. Polk's presidency she went, as she often did, to take Mrs. Madison for a drive. The servant returned to the carriage with the message that Mrs. Madison was engaged with company, and that she wished Mrs. Polk would come in. Entering the parlor, she found a group of ladies with whom she had interchanged visits when her husband was a member of Congress. They immediately began to complain playfully that she did not return their calls, saying, "Now, Mrs. Polk, we have you before Mrs. Madison, and we are going to try you. Now, Mrs. Madison, we leave it to you; don't you think so young a lady as Mrs. Polk ought to return visits, and come to see us as she used to do? Did you not return calls and make visits when you were in the White House?" "Yes, my children, I did," said the venerable widow; "but one parlor would then contain all who came to my receptions. How could the

people come to Washington in those days? There
were no railroads, and there were stage-lines only
from New York and Baltimore and Richmond.
There were even no turnpikes. And the people
would not come in their carriages. Now there are
so many people in the city that it is an impossibility to return the calls that are made on the
President's household."

Mrs. Polk said, " I gave up the custom of returning calls, because it soon became plain to me that I
could not visit without making discriminations, and
that would inevitably give offence."

A gentleman, in talking with her of his parents
whom she had known forty years before, asked how
it was that we so seldom in these days meet with
persons like them, eminent for intelligence and refinement. "It is," she replied, "because of the
great diffusion, in the present time, of education
and knowledge, and the universal advancement of
the country. Everybody knows more, and there
are therefore fewer persons eminent for knowledge
and cultivation. Many years ago it was only the
rich who could be educated, and therefore there
were comparatively few eligible to office and political appointment. They continued for years in official position because through experience they became thoroughly conversant with their duties, and

were fully competent to discharge them. As a rule, they were also men of sound principles and integrity. Now, men are more generally competent to hold office, and more easily get into places of honor and trust, and," she added, "they are more easily turned out by others. And, somehow, many men are not governed by the upright, stern principles of former days."

A few days before Christmas, 1885, we saw her in her own room. Some one had asked for information from her concerning Mr. Polk's conduct of the Mexican war, and she was beginning to make notes of what she could recall.

A friend had sent her a wood-cut, clipped from a newspaper, of the log house, near Charlotte, North Carolina, in which her husband was born. It was a fac-simile of the primitive abodes in which so many noted persons began life. The picture was lying in a large copy of the New Testament and Psalms which rested on the broad arm of her easy-chair. Looking with interest into the well-worn volume, one of us read some of the marked passages. She spoke of the pleasure the sacred writings gave her, and said, "Did you ever notice the correspondence between the ninetieth and the ninety-first Psalms? The latter seems, verse by verse, to answer the former."

Referring to her husband's abstemiousness and the hard work which had cut short his life, she said that she herself was in the habit of eating but little. When the kindness of her nieces and the attentiveness of her servants pressed her to partake more freely, she told them that she was satisfied, and that it was unseemly for one who was waiting for her last order to be thinking of eating and drinking. Then, with a burst of feeling, she exclaimed, " My whole heart is a thank-offering; and I am ready to go when the mandate comes." Smilingly she spoke of having attended church after a long enforced absence, and of the good sermon of her pastor, Dr. Witherspoon, from the text, " And the door was shut." She was impressed with the beautiful singing, in which her young niece took part. She said that in this country and in Europe there were clergymen of ability and education who, in the perhaps unconscious desire to show their learning, had lost the guidance of faith, and were confused in the labyrinth of error. On one occasion, when seated at a diplomatic dinner at the White House, and attended by M. de Bodisco, the eldest foreign representative, she spoke of having been present at a certain religious service. The Russian ambassador, who of course was a member of the Greek Church, said to her, " Why did you go to hear that man, Madame?

Why do you care to hear a man tell of things that you can learn without him, and that you know as well as he does?" She replied simply with the question, "What do you do in your church, Mr. Bodisco?" "We go to church, Madame, to worship."

She was much grieved by the tragic death of Mrs. Pendleton, of Ohio, who was thrown from her carriage in Central Park, New York, and instantly killed. Mrs. Pendleton was the daughter of Francis Scott Key, and Mrs. Polk recalled her friendship with the writer of our grand national hymn. He used often to visit Representative Polk and his wife, in their boarding-house; and the ladies of the house would say to her, " I get tired of staying in the parlor so long, but I wish very much to see ' Star-Spangled Banner; ' do please let me know in some way when he comes."

The marriage of President Cleveland called forth a brief letter of congratulation. Accompanying the modest announcement of the wedding of "Mr. Grover Cleveland and Miss Frances Folsom," she received a piece of the wedding-cake, wrapped in silver paper and lace, and enclosed in a little white satin box on which, in gilt letters, was the date of the auspicious event, and a card bearing the autographs of the bride and bridegroom.

One evening in August Mrs. Polk told us an incident in her early married life, when she and her husband were travelling from Columbia to Murfreesborough. They went in their own carriage, and the route lay through Franklin and Triune. The rains had been heavy and the rivers and creeks were high. About ten or twelve miles from Franklin they came to a creek so dangerous to ford that they hesitated. While considering what to do, a man approached them from a long lane opening into the road, and with cordial salutations advised them not to attempt a passage of the turbulent waters, and pressingly invited them to wait at his house near by until they could proceed safely on their journey. He was a wealthy farmer, and their stay with his family from Friday until Monday was remembered as a pleasant episode in their changeful lives. One of the daughters was a mute, and she took a fancy to a bead reticule carried by Mrs. Polk according to the custom of that day. She would gaze at it, and drawing near, would point out the vari-colored flowers to the others, and talk rapidly to them in signs and finger-language. Just before leaving, Mrs. Polk took her handkerchief and purse out of the bag, and smoothing the ribbons, and wrapping it in a piece of paper, she presented it to the young girl. Her delight was enthusiastic, and she spelled out this sentence, which was interpreted to the gentle and gracious guest, " I will pray for you."

In the summer of 1887 Miss Fall went to Europe with a few friends. Frequent letters from abroad enabled Mrs. Polk, from her loop-hole of retreat, to see many interesting scenes in the old world, through the eyes of her niece.

Speaking one day of the great change in public sentiment regarding the respectability of labor, now nearly the opposite of what it was forty years ago, she said: " It is beautiful to see how women are supporting themselves, and how those who go forward independently in various callings are respected and admired for their energy and industry. It is now considered proper for young ladies, when they leave school, to teach or to do something else for themselves. It was not so in my young days. When we were in Washington an estimable lady, who with her husband successfully conducted a large school, was invited to visit us at the White House, with her pupils. She said to me, ' Mrs. Polk, this is the first time I have ever been invited to the White House !' Though a woman of culture and high character, her occupation of school-teaching barred her from social equality."

Whenever she was not able to attend the public celebration of the Lord's Supper, she read the Scrip-

17

ture passages referring to the Supper, and the beautiful Episcopal service in the prayer-book. Showing us a small volume for daily devotions, called "The Watches," she said that Bishop Otey gave it to her a few weeks after Mr. Polk's death. It was marked and underscored, and much worn with use, and had been re-bound. She said the Psalms were a great delight to her, and the day seemed incomplete when she had failed to read one or more of them.

In July, 1888, a telegram in the morning paper announced the death of Rev. Dr. Riddle, who had been pastor of a church in Pittsburg for fifty years. This brought to Mrs. Polk's remembrance a Sabbath she had long ago spent in that city. The rain was pouring, and Mr. Polk thought the day too inclement for her to go out. Mr. Campbell, of Albany, who was travelling with them, proposed to order a carriage, but she declined. However, when the hour arrived he was at the door, and they drove to the church together and had the pleasure of hearing Dr. Riddle preach.

Dr. Rubey, of Clinton, Missouri, wrote to Mrs. Polk concerning the authorship of an anonymous book presented to him some years before by Judge Caruthers, of Lebanon, Tennessee. It is a small muslin-bound volume entitled "Monterey Conquered," published in New York, in 1852. It is an epic poem, with Roman names distinguishing the American characters, reminding one of the fashion formerly followed by sculptors of disguising modern statesmen in the Roman toga. It contains some fine passages and beautiful similes, and is pervaded by a lofty spirit, not always equalled by grace of expression. President Polk, General Taylor, General Scott, and others prominent in the stirring scenes of the Mexican war, are the principal figures; and fictitious events and characters are mingled with the real, after the manner of historical romancists. She had no recollection of the volume or of its author.

On one rainy Saturday she brought out a gilded morocco case, within which, on a red velvet lining dulled with age, lay a costly fan, saying that General Pillow had presented it to her at the close of the Mexican war. The pearl strips of the handle, gleaming with soft opaline tints, were ornamented with open-work and gilding. "It is too heavy for use," she said. "I carried it only on state occasions." Not long afterward she gave to a daughter of General Pillow's this beautiful remembrance of her father.

From her home in St. Louis, Mrs. Dr. Brown wrote thus to a friend in Nashville : —

"Ask Mrs. Polk if she remembers their ride from Washington, Pennsylvania, to Brownsville, in a stage-coach, on the way to the White House, when her husband was to become the President of the United States; and if she recalls a little black-eyed school-girl who by mistake had seated herself in the decorated presidential coach — large as life. When the President and his wife were handed in she wished to vacate, as she saw the gravity of her mistake, but dear Mrs. Polk said, ' No, keep your seat.' When the stage stopped for dinner Mrs. Polk, out of the kindness of that generous heart of hers, said, ' You are our guest, and will dine with us.' That little girl has never forgotten the gracious treatment bestowed upon her on that day, and only a few weeks ago was telling it all over; and now I tell it to you, and you must tell it to Mrs. Polk. That little girl is my own dear cousin, and bears my mother's name. Her father was a Whig, but that did not interfere with her enjoyment; to be the guest of President Polk and his wife was a great honor, with which party had nothing to do."

When Mrs. Polk was eighty-six years old, she received the following remembrance: —

WASHINGTON, SEPTEMBER, 1889.

My DEAR MRS. POLK, — Your birthday returns, and your friends are happy in your continued

health and enjoyment of life. As the oldest of
them, and as one who, if spared, will in a few days
enter on his ninetieth year, I congratulate you on
your health and vigor. May the coming year be
one of perfect health and happiness to you; you
hold the affectionate regard of your country, and
the esteem and best wishes of a nation minister
to your length of days better than all the efforts and
care of the men of the healing art can do. There
is a constant refreshment of life in enjoying the
highest esteem and regard of a free people, who
elected your husband to be their chief, and who enabled him to fill his years of office with the greatest
deeds. Live long, that you may more and more see
the astonishing results of his administrative genius.
Count me ever as one of the most earnest of your
friends, — perhaps the truest as the oldest of them
all. Ever with affectionate respect,

Your devoted friend,

George Bancroft.

Speaking of her refusal to give to friends letters
of recommendation for office, addressed to the
President, she said she had always declined the
repeated requests for such letters. She reasoned
that should she give such a recommendation, and
the applicant for office be successful, it would be

heralded over the country that she was now med-
dling with politics. This would not only increase
the number of such applications, but would have
the effect of making her recommendations annoying, and render her liable to the loss of whatever
influence she might possess. " Besides," she said,
" in my opinion, it is undignified to make such
solicitations; and in scores of cases I have politely
declined to do what old friends and acquaintances
have urgently asked. I have maintained this position through all the years from 1849 to the present
time, though it was often painful to refuse valued
friends."

Few indeed have been the women who continued
to receive poetical tributes after passing the allotted
bound of three-score years and ten. Christmas
Day, 1889, brought her an acrostic-sonnet from
General McAdoo, of Knoxville. In the note accompanying it he wrote, " Its prime commenda-
tion is that it truly expresses my feelings toward
you."

TO THE ILLUSTRIOUS MRS. EX-PRESIDENT POLK.

> Loved relict of our nation's ruler pure,
>   Oh, bless thee that thy life hath spanned the years,
>   Vexed not by time's decline, and still appears
> Exalted toward fame's summit yet more sure !
> Deep-graven history shall through time endure ;

Washington D.C.
27 April 1887.

Dear Mrs Polk

It was an honor for me to meet
you again; a joy to find you so well; the highest
satisfaction to agree with you in one common
reverence for the President whom I shall
never cease to honor. If you can & will
entrust to me his papers, I will devote every
moment to them till I return them, & I think
I could return them in three or in two weeks, or in less.

Best regards to your household; I ought to
have imposed on Mr Fall the generous office of his good
advice & sharp eyes in selecting a Riding Horse.
I am ever, dear Mrs Polk,
very devotedly yours
Geo. Bancroft

So with thy noble husband's rule long years
All impotent defies ; and ceaseless cheers
Rewards shall to his deathless fame assure !
As Helena, illustrious, in bright glow,
　Her sunset years enjoyed when her great son,
　Proud Constantine, proclaimed that Christ is King,
Oh, ever thus thy vigor pleaseth so !
Life's mortal still is blest ; and when all 's done,
Kings no translation loftier can show !

Referring often to the friends who had ever been ready to advise and assist her in business affairs, she mentioned many names with grateful regard. Her acquaintance with Mr. Anson Nelson began when he was the tax collector of the city, before the Civil War. Judge Catron urged her to consult him about her financial affairs. "He told me," she said, "that I needed some prudent adviser who could be seen at any time; and as Major Graham had removed to the country, and he himself was away from Nashville more than half the time, holding court in other States, it was necessary to have other advisers. So, at my request, Mr. Nelson called to see me regularly once a week. During the war, when no business advice was needed, he was accustomed to call on Sunday afternoons, and has kept up the habit ever since, to my gratification."

Through the winter of 1889-1890, we were received in her own room. She always took part in the conversation, and was specially interested in all that related to the old days. Her thoughts seemed to be gradually weaned from subjects that had long interested her, — even from politics. Occasionally a little flicker of enthusiasm for some man or some measure would flare, and then she would sigh and say, " I don't care for these things. Why should I? I am astonished at myself that I am here, when nearly all the friends of my younger days are gone." She would then repeat with evident pleasure some incident of the former times, thus pleasing her visitors as well as herself.

One day she said that years ago, while there was sitting with her a lady of high integrity and of an intelligence above the average, yet of such stern and strict candor that by many her friendship was dreaded rather than enjoyed, several gentlemen were announced. These visitors were eminent men, lawyers, judges, preachers, and the spokesman a scientist of repute, but somewhat peculiar in his personal appearance. When they had taken their departure this lady asked her, " Why do you receive visits from those men? And why do you wish to talk to a man who is filled with vanity, pride, and ambition? It is unbecoming a Christian to do so." " Mrs. Blank," was the reply, " I have never sought anything for myself. I have been placed where I am by a higher power; for the Bible says, 'Promotion cometh neither from the east, nor from the west, nor from the south. But God is the judge; He putteth down one, and setteth up another.' And if I did not accept the visits of professional men, ministers of the gospel, as well as others, it would be a pretence of being a better Christian woman than I am." To this reply, from her own standpoint, the lady could offer no objection.

The day before her eighty-seventh birthday the Rev. Dr. Whitsitt thus wrote to a mutual friend concerning his kinswoman: " It is matter of rejoicing that her health and spirits are so fine, at her advanced age. I trust that she will be spared yet many years. Her lively religious hope has been a strong comfort to her, and it has often edified me to hear her speak of the value she set upon the prospects of a higher world. In this whole world there are not many such . elevated and noble characters. I honor her without any reserve."

During this summer Mrs. Polk received from Mrs. ex-Governor Perry of South Carolina, a niece of Gen. Robert Y. Hayne, several volumes which contained valuable writings of her deceased husband. Benjamin Franklin Perry was Provisional

Governor of South Carolina in 1865. There was no organized government in the State at the time, and no legal protection for life, liberty, or property. Although the claims of several other prominent citizens were presented to President Johnson, he saw proper to appoint Mr. Perry. At the close of the year the State government was re-organized. The correspondence between Mrs. Polk and Mrs. Perry, carried on for the former by the hand of a friend, was interesting to the two widows whose husbands had taken so active a part in the affairs of their country.

When a letter announced that Mrs. Polk had been elected an honorary vice-president of the Daughters of the American Revolution, she accepted the compliment with appreciation and pleasure, — " extremely grateful," she said, " to be associated with such an order."

New Year's Day, 1891, brought a pleasant greeting from an old and tried friend : —

LEALAND, Jan. 1, 1891.

MRS. JAMES K. POLK: DEAR MADAME, — The weather is so inclement that I have to deprive myself of the very great pleasure of paying to you my annual visit, but I send my greetings and give to you all the good wishes of the season.

For more than the length of years allotted to the average life of man or woman, on the anniversary of this day, with scarcely a single omission, have I visited your hospitable home; and though absent on this occasion, I beg that you will consider me as one of the numerous friends who will call to pay to you their respects. Sidney Smith says, "One is all the happier for having once been happy," and judging by that standard, who more blessed than you, or who more grateful for the blessing? Your life, dear Madame, has been dimmed only by a single cloud, only one real grief, and that comes sooner or later to every household; *death* enters every hovel and every palace. All else with you has been only what heart could wish, — honor, respect, and "troops of friends." May blessings always accompany you, and, though aged, may you yet linger many years above the horizon; such is my greeting. Very sincerely,

JOHN M. LEA.

Judge Lea's father, Luke Lea, was in Congress with Mr. Polk, and on one of their returns homeward Mr. Lea prevailed upon Mr. and Mrs. Polk to rest at his country home at Campbell's Station, fifteen miles west of Knoxville. This mansion, situated on a high hill, and shaded with grand old trees, commanded a wide and beautiful prospect. When Mr. Polk died, in 1849, Judge Lea was mayor of Nashville. Interments within city limits were not allowed, except by special permission, and Mrs. Polk sent to him to obtain the necessary order to build the tomb on her own grounds. Instead of sending a messenger, or a letter, he came himself, and kindly and courteously offered his services, while granting the desired permission in the name of the city.

On the 17th of January George Bancroft passed away, in his ninety-first year. Standing herself so near the boundary of life, her affections naturally turned from the past, and became fixed more and more upon the future now lying just beyond. She was not therefore deeply moved by the earthly loss of this true friend of well-nigh half a century.

It gave her pleasure to receive about this time a poem entitled, " Reminiscences of the Polk Mansion," written by Mrs. C., of Massachusetts. This lady had been an invalid for nineteen years, and wrote the lines in her sick chamber, knowing Polk Place only through the medium of a newspaper article describing a visit to that interesting house.

In March Mrs. Polk had a severe illness, from

which, however, she recovered in a few weeks. Her moderation in all things, her quiet contentment, and above all, her habitual submission to the Divine will, contributed to an early restoration which was a surprise to all. With her wonted spirit of serenity, she said that she was not half grateful enough for the goodness which had been showered upon her all her life. She also spoke of her light-hearted happiness, freedom from care, and exemption from severe discipline, and quoted various passages from her favorite Psalms. She said that she had not cared for society life, and had not entered its charmed circle in Nashville. "No, Madame," it was returned, "you have gone out only to church." "Yes," she replied, "and received the visits of those who came to honor the character of my husband, which was very great. I have not sought anything. I have not travelled. I have remained at home, and received what came to me. And I am satisfied with it, and am not anxious for anything more. I am content now to be the old woman declining in life, and waiting the Almighty's orders, and to accept His way of directing my days. God is good. I am thankful. My heart is filled with joy."

Concerning the approaching nuptials of her young niece, she remarked, "Saidee wishes to be married at home; and she says that if I am not able to witness the ceremony in the parlor she will be married right here at my bedside." The marriage took place on the twelfth of May. It was a brilliant home wedding, in the large parlor, and Mrs. Polk was present.

THE PEACEFUL AND TRIUM-
PHANT END.

CHAPTER XVI.

1891.

ALTHOUGH growing feebler day after day, and disinclined even to the slight exertion of getting into a carriage, nevertheless, in the sultry August weather Mrs. Polk rode out three afternoons in succession. On returning home on Wednesday, the 12th of August, she sat a little while in her accustomed place in the hall, talking with the family in her usual bright strain. As she went to her room, leaning on her servant's arm, her strength suddenly failed. She seemed very ill, and immediately lay down, instead of partaking of the supper which had been spread for her on a little table beside her easy-chair. The next morning the family were at first greatly encouraged, believing her to be much better. But it was soon evident that the wonderful vitality was ebbing away. There were intervals of suffering throughout the day, and the succeeding night. Life was now surely going out. On Friday morn-

ing, just before daybreak, the doctors who had
been in attendance upon her were hastily summoned. As one of them entered the room he
informed the family that the end was very near.
She said to her niece, " Sallie, if you will let
me turn over, I will try to get a little sleep."
Mrs. Fall, who was kneeling by the bedside, replied in trembling tones, " Aunt Sarah, the last
long sleep, for which you have been waiting, is
very near. That is the sleep which will soon
come to refresh you." She looked at her niece
quietly as these words fell from her lips, but
seemed a little surprised that the departure she
had been expecting daily for many years had at
last come with so brief a warning. Then she
said, in the calm, clear voice familiar and dear
to them all, " Well, I am ready. I am willing
to go. Praise God from whom all blessings flow!"

Mrs. Fall, bending over her, said, " Darling, do
you love me?" "I do, I do," was the emphatic
response. "We have lived together a long time,
peacefully and happily." Then, softly, distinctly,
earnestly, she repeated the words of thankful
submission and joyous praise which had so long
dwelt in her heart, and ever ready to break forth.
She reiterated her unshaken trust in God, quoting
the passages of Scripture that had sustained her

hope; and also began to repeat certain lines from her favorite hymn, " I would not live alway." This outflow of feeling continued but for a little while, as her strength was waning every moment. But the strong, beautiful intellect remained undimmed. It was nearly seven o'clock when, placing upon her niece's head the soft hands, now cold with the chill of approaching death, she pronounced a blessing which seemed like the benediction of a bishop: " The Lord bless thee, and keep thee, and make His face shine upon thee, and give thee happiness and love and everlasting peace ! "

It was her last utterance. She lay quite still, breathing naturally. A slight sound came from her lips, and the name " Sallie" was feebly whispered, but nothing further could be understood. As the clock in the hall struck half-past seven, the faint breath ceased, and she passed into the Better Country.

In the absence of her pastor, the Rev. Dr. Witherspoon, the Rev. Mr. McNeilly had been sent for. Living a little distance from the city, he did not reach Polk Place until the spirit had taken its flight.

The flags on the State and Federal buildings were placed at half-mast; and the solemn tolling of the bells of the city, stroke after stroke, in slow succession, gave expression to the sorrow of the community among whom had lived for nearly half a century this stately woman of the olden time.

Mr. B. G. Wood, the president of the local Association of Mexican Veterans, wrote: " We are anxious to pay our last respects to the noble woman who presided at the White House while we were in the service of our country in a foreign nation, and her husband was the Commander-in-Chief of our army and navy. Mrs. Polk has been the idol of the veterans for many years, and they always met a hearty greeting from her."

The " American" in its next issue voiced the general sentiment: —

" All the people of Tennessee grieve as the news goes forth that Mrs. James K. Polk is dead. Full of years and of honors, rich in the devotion and tender affection of her household, and in the deep and universal esteem of Tennesseans, the end of life came peacefully, — not as to one whom the infirmities of age and the forgetfulness of friends has made weary of the world, but as to one blessed in all earthly surroundings, and blessed in the sublime serenity of a Christian's faith. Conscious of the waning vitality which warned her of the approach of death, she has waited for the summons with cheerfulness and patience. It is needless to dwell upon the character of Mrs. Polk, — the intellectual mind undimmed to the end, the unfailing gentleness which continued to the close, the loyal heart which cherished to the last the memory of the great man whose life was blessed with her constant devotion and faithful help. It is a positive blessing to this generation that this noble woman was spared to bring to bear upon it the beautiful character-istics and the splendid mental and heart training which were hers in a measure that can be said of few women. The South will for generations to come recall proudly her memory and point with profound pride to her career."

The following letter was sent from the Executive office at the State House: —

NASHVILLE, Aug. 14.

To THE FAMILY AND FRIENDS OF MRS. SARAH
    CHILDRESS POLK :

On the part of the State of Tennessee, I desire to extend sympathy in this bereavement. I feel that not only the State, but the nation, has sus-tained a loss in the death of so refined, so cultured, so noble a woman as Mrs. Polk, the widow of one of Tennessee's greatest, best-beloved sons and the nation's most exalted chieftains, James K. Polk. She has stood a peer among the women of the land, a perfect type of the gentle woman-hood of the old South, and her influence will live forever. The State of Tennessee will hold no spot more hallowed than that which has the honor to contain the remains of this distinguished son and his gentle wife, and will ever give all honor to their memory. With great respect, I beg leave to subscribe myself your obedient servant,

JOHN P. BUCHANAN, *Governor.*

Adjutant-General Norman proffered the family a military escort and guard, which was courteously and gratefully declined, in compliance with Mrs. Polk's desire for perfect simplicity in the funeral services.

The body lay in the chamber where she had slept for two and forty years, her niece saying that she could not let it be carried into the lonely parlor. In accordance with Mrs. Polk's request, a white silk winding-sheet was wrapped about her, similar to the one in which her husband was buried. The sweet, dignified features bore an expression of peace and rest. It seemed as if she had just fallen asleep and would soon waken and speak again.

Telegrams continued to come in for several days from all parts of the country. One was sent by Judge Lea, from Maine, where he was sojourning: "The death of Mrs. Polk removes from me a lifetime friend. Deeply do I, and deeply does Tennessee sympathize with her afflicted family." The Rev. Dr. Witherspoon, absent in Washington, sent the following: "Have just heard of your sorrow.

Accept my profound sympathy." The Hon. James
D. Richardson, a member of Congress from Tennessee, telegraphed from Minneapolis to Capt. John
W. Childress: "Please tender assurances of my
sympathy to the family of Mrs. Polk. I would
attend burial if physically able." Colonel McClure,
of Philadelphia, sent the following: "Mrs. McClure
joins me in sincerest expressions of sorrow at the
announcement of Mrs. Polk's death. Her memory
will ever be enshrined in the country's love." A
cablegram from London brought "Sympathy!"
from the Hon. Thomas D. Craighead and Dr.
William L. Nichol.

The city press gave details of the event, full of
pathetic interest. "The Daily Herald" said: —

"No stress is laid upon the magnificence of the flowers;
but the small posy of delicate, old-fashioned blooms,
which Miss Thomas (an aged and life-long friend) brought
in her own hands, was given the place of highest honor
within the still white clasp of those hands which have
never known but to do good. The great stone doors of
the tomb shall close upon the quaint cluster of flowers
modestly and sweetly adorning the great lady's hands, and
the token shall be eternal.

"One of the most beautiful stories which comes to light
in connection with the death is the attachment of the venerable Anson Nelson and his wife to the lady whose husband figured so prominently in the stirring political scenes
which made memorable the earlier days of his residence

here. It has long been their custom to visit her every
Sabbath afternoon, and to engage in an hour of Christian
conversation. When it was impossible for them to see
her, they proved their constant devotion by writing a letter
to her upon the subjects nearest their hearts. And when
the news reached them that the friend of so many years
had passed away, they immediately left their brother's home
in Asheville, North Carolina, and with heavy hearts hastened
upon a journey which meant such a sad ending to them
of ties faithfully cherished."

Mr. Cornelius, who had charge of the funeral,
performed the same service for Mr. Polk, forty-two
years before. It was thought that Sunday morning
was " the sweetest time," and the last sad rites
therefore took place at nine o'clock on that day.
An old lady from the country, who came early, said
as she looked into the large south parlor where the
flower-designs were grouped about the casket in
rich profusion, " This is not a funeral. This looks
like heaven." Many persons came from the adja-
cent towns and counties, and from all classes of
society, the poor and humble and obscure, as well
as the wealthy and prominent. The services were
conducted by Rev. Dr. Price, of the Presbyterian
University at Clarksville, assisted by Rev. Dr.
Steel, pastor of the McKendree Methodist Church,
and the Rev. J. H. McNeilly. After prayer and
Scripture-reading, and the singing of several hymns,

one of which was her favorite, " I would not live
alway," Mr. McNeilly delivered a beautiful and appropriate discourse.   He had examined Mrs. Polk's
daily companions, the "Watches," and the New
Testament which lay on the broad arm of her easy-
chair, and from the marked passages therein had
formed a just estimate of her spiritual life and
character.

Among the pall-bearers were four elders of her
own church, and Colonel Claiborne, who was a
bearer at the ex-President's funeral in 1849.   The
procession passed from the house to the tomb, and
the casket was lowered into the vault, and placed
beside the casket of her husband.   After prayer
and a benediction, the family and friends withdrew,
and the multitude had an opportunity to pass and
look into the tomb.   During all the services the
city bells were tolling a solemn requiem.

In a letter to the family, Dr. Witherspoon
wrote : —

" My distress at the intelligence it is impossible
for me to express.   Along with that sorrow was a
feeling of sincere regret that as her pastor, and
yours, I was so far away, and thus providentially
deprived of the privilege of witnessing an end so
peaceful and triumphant, and of giving you what of
consolation I might have been able.   I shall always

be happy and proud in the thought that Mrs. Polk
was my friend, and that I bore to her the sacred
relation of pastor. It is a sweet satisfaction to
know that her confidence I enjoyed while she yet
lingered with us to brighten our lives by her
womanly worth and her noble Christian character.
. . . I can well imagine what a change in your life,
and in that of your loved ones, is made by her
going from you. We all know how she loved the
inmates of that home, who tenderly loved her in
return, and ministered to her so faithfully in the
evening of her precious life. He who rewards the
giving of a cup of cold water in His name to one
of His disciples, will surely recompense you and
yours for smoothing her path to the grave. May
the God of all grace who took the sting out of
death for her, bless and comfort you."

Judge Lea wrote: "Her friendship for me was
one of the treasures of my life."

From an article in the "American" we extract
the following paragraph: —

"She was a true woman and a strong woman; true to
all the best feelings of a warm and honest heart; strong in
all that belongs to a cultivated mind, and a brave one. She
had strength of purpose, a clear intellect, and was a wise
and sagacious student of affairs, not only because she had
the mind to comprehend and appreciate, but also because

she tenderly revered the memory of her husband, who had been honored with the highest gifts by the people of his country. She was a great woman, and few have lived like her ; for she passed unscathed through an ordeal that few women and men, living or dead, could have passed, and left a bright record behind them."

The following inscription has been placed on the west side of the tomb, in the place originally left vacant for this purpose : —

ASLEEP IN JESUS.

———

MRS. SARAH CHILDRESS POLK,

WIFE OF

JAMES KNOX POLK.

BORN IN RUTHERFORD COUNTY, TENN.,
SEPT. 4, 1803.

DIED AT POLK PLACE, NASHVILLE, TENN.,
AUGUST 14, 1891.

———

A noble woman, a devoted wife,
a true friend, a sincere Christian.

———

"Blessed are the dead which die in the Lord."

These memorials may fitly close with the following letter, addressed to Mrs. Fall : —

EVANSTON, ILL., Aug. 15, 1891.

DEAR FRIEND, — A noble Christian and typical American lady of the old school has gone from this world, and a beloved aunt and household comrade has left your historic home. Seeing Mrs. Polk first in 1881, I have omitted no opportunity to do so when in Nashville since then. The portrait at the White House, placed there by American women, Northern and Southern, was a beautiful token of our renewed love and good understanding. The Christian example of Mrs. President Polk at the Executive Mansion will brighten the annals of our common country. These lines cannot express the full measure of appreciation and reverence that I have always cherished for your illustrious aunt. Well might the church bells toll for one always loyal to our Lord, and the flags be placed at half-mast for a patriot who dignified the name " American." May God's blessing be with you all who loved her, and who have lost her out of your lives, is the prayer of

Yours in the love of God and of Humanity,

FRANCES E. WILLARD.